BLACK STUDIES

RAP

AND THE ACADEMY

HOUSTON A. BAKER, JR.

The University of Chicago Press • Chicago and London

Portions of chapter 3 were previously published in
Gina Dent, ed., *Black Popular Culture* (Seattle: Bay
Press, 1993); portions of chapter 4 were published,
in an earlier form, in Constance Penley and Andrew
Ross, eds., *Technoculture* (Minneapolis: University of
Minnesota Press, 1991).

The University of Chicago Press, Chicago 60637
The University of Chicago Press, Ltd., London
© 1993 by Houston A. Baker, Jr.
All rights reserved. Published 1993
Paperback edition 1995
Printed in the United States of America

02 01 00 99 98 97 96 95   2345
ISBN: 0-226-03520-4 (cloth)
ISBN: 0-226-03521-2 (paper)

Library of Congress Cataloging-in-Publication Data

Baker, Houston A.
    Black studies, rap, and the academy / Houston
A. Baker, Jr.
        p.   cm. — (Black literature and culture)
    1. Afro-Americans—Study and teaching
(Higher)   2. Afro-Americans—Education.   3.
United States—Popular culture.   4. Rap (Music)—
History and criticism.   I. Title.   II. Series.
E184.7.B3   1993
973'.0496073'00711—dc20   92-42997
                                            CIP

The primary focus of Unity Weekend celebrations over the past twelve years has been the family—a rededication of family values, morals, and social interaction. The Unity experience was born in 1978 as the need for family reunification became a pressing concern to the management of WDAS AM/FM. Over the years it has grown from 50,000 in attendance to last year's *record-setting 800,000.*

> From the Unity Day marketing
> brochure of the sponsor of the celebration,
> a Black Philadelphia Radio Station

Let the beat hit 'em,
Let the music take control!

CONTENTS

PREFACE

The present essay is the result of a short-term visiting fellowship at Princeton University. Professor Arnold Rampersad of American Studies and Professor Victor Brombert of the Council of the Humanities graciously invited me to present lectures as a Whitney J. Oates Fellow during the spring of 1992. My topic was the relationship between black urban influences and the formation of Black Studies during the 1960s; I was concerned as well with the relationship of one contemporary form of black urban culture, namely rap music and poetry, to contemporary black academics. The guiding idea of my reflections was the coextensiveness of "inside" and "out" in the actual process of Black Studies' founding. This idea was expanded to include the interrelations between the "outside" expressive cultural energies of today's black urban youth and contemporary scholars "inside" the academy. If my understanding of contemporary cultural studies is correct, considerations of such inside/outside negotiations constitute part of that project's work.

But I do not wish to make grandiose claims for the reflections that follow. They are not meant as local recapit-
ulations of global intellectual work from Gramsci and
Adorno, through Williams and Hebdige, gathering
steam from Birmingham and Champaign-Urbana in the
process. Rather, they are designed as re-vocabulariza-
tions, resettings, and expansions, as it were, of inside/
outside scholarly and creative energies that have mightily influenced the American academy during the past
two and one half decades. They represent merely a single installment on a large debt to be paid to the past
and a modest analytical investment in Black Studies fu-
tures. Finally, they offer a critique of what seems to be
a compromising moment in a worthwhile mission begun
many years ago. They conclude with a "sounding" of
rap that suggests a possible model of appreciation and
understanding for tomorrow's Black Studies scholars.

My thanks are extended, as always, to my wife Char-
lotte Pierce-Baker, who has been a gracious and astute
critic of this project from its inception. And though all
thanks do not remain "in the family," a healthy share of
my gratitude belongs to my son Mark Frederick Baker,
who worked as a truly remarkable research assistant in
shaping this project. Ruth Lindeborg and Joann Hippo-
lyte also provided research assistance.

Professor Manthia Diawara read portions of the man-
uscript and provided excellent suggestions for improve-
ment. Audiences at Princeton, Purdue, Kenyon, Am-
herst, and Dickinson all offered extremely profitable
responses and corrections. Finally, a word of profound
gratitude goes out to all the cultural workers who

"brought the noise" that launched the Black Studies
project. And "peace" to the rappers—the black poets
of the contemporary urban scene, who at times seem to
be the last voices in America talking bravely back and
black in these new times.

1

BLACK STUDIES: A NEW STORY

The single task that I set myself for the summer of 1991 was an essay on Black Studies and the institution of English. I was less certain about English in its daily, postmodern unfoldings than I was about Black Studies, for who can ever be certain what is happening at Duke? By contrast, everyone knows the familiar story of Black Studies. It is a narrative of Hagar's children redeemed from exile by the grace of affirmative action and the intentionality of Black Power. It is a vernacular tale, resonant with rhythm and blues. And it has been relegated in recent years to the briefest imaginable space in the encyclopedia of postmodern American academics. Thus it was that, in the summer of 1991, I wanted to construct a Black Studies account that would produce, perhaps, a conclusion rather different from "Negroes also spoke." I hoped, in short, to avoid "soul" narration.

A number of factors converged, however, to make my job more complicated than I had envisioned. First, the currents of the PC (Political Correctness) Cavaliers were

swirling, during the summer of 1991, with the energy
of Edgar Allan Poe's maelstrom. Everywhere one turned,
after the Modern Language Association opposed the nom-
ination of Carol Iannone to the National Council on
the Humanities, there were editorials and "op. ed."
meditations denouncing a new "leftism" of "tenured rad-
icals" in the American academy. Professors who suggested that Alice Walker might conceivably form part
of a course devoted to American literature were held to
be equivalent—in the bizarre logic of the PC Cavaliers—to Ku Klux Klanspersons. (Don't ask me to explain it.) And in the economies of the PC Cavaliers,
Black Studies was just one more roundheaded carryover
from the chaotic 1960s, when mere anarchy was loosed
in halls of ivy. Like other interdisciplinary area studies
(e.g., Women's Studies) to which it lent force, Black
Studies was suddenly being held accountable for a new
"McCarthyism." (Again, don't ask me to explain it—
at least not yet.)

There thus seemed to be at least two incumbencies
if I were going to achieve a new and different story.
I would certainly have to account for the new politics
of PC by, at least, re-vocabularizing the familiar Black
Studies tale to avoid its easy imbrication in a simple-
minded, right-wing rhetoric of denunciation. Second,
since Black Studies was founded as a social, scholarly,
and pedagogical enterprise to deal with black culture, I
would have to account for the relationship of such studies to black urban culture. Black urban culture, I believe, provided much of the impetus for Black Studies's

founding, and surely in our own era, it is the locus of quite extraordinary transnational creative energy.

Having arrived at the contours of my narrative mission, I had absolutely no clear idea of how to fulfill it. I felt like Mr. Phelps in the original run of *Mission Impossible:* I was out "in the cold," and the scholarly muses had disavowed knowledge of my proper person. In such instances, there is no recourse but improvisation. So I found myself by midsummer trying to follow the unfolding PC debates, struggling to read cultural studies materials, and carving out time to catch up on the black urban expressivity of *Yo! MTV Raps.* This welter of anxiety and influences produced such hybrid moments as putting aside the *Wall Street Journal*'s latest diatribe against PC to take up the writings of Paul Gilroy while listening, with one ear, to the jamming lyrics of Ice-T's unbelievable *OG* (Original Gangster) album. Having concluded that the notion of "nation," as employed and analyzed by Black British cultural studies, was indispensable to my narrative, I set out on a sunny Sunday in August to borrow a copy of Benedict Anderson's *Imagined Communities* from a friend who lives near Philadelphia's Benjamin Franklin Parkway. Instead of Anderson's book, I quite serendipitously discovered an energetically imagined community of interests in action, one that seemed rather like a Wordsworthian spot of time.

It was Unity Day on the Parkway. Thousands of people were assembled, and the scene seemed to offer—in its collaged multiplicity of sound and image—a fore-

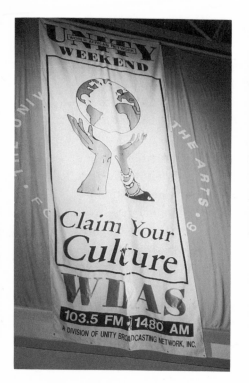 

Unity Weekend 1992. Photographs courtesy WDAS Radio, Philadelphia.

shadowing of both the form and substance I hoped to capture in my new story of Black Studies. But I knew immediately that no written text could fully capture the gorgeously arrayed young black people in African-print shirts and dresses set off by roped-gold jewelry and kofi hats. Nor could academic writing make readers feel the heat and stillness as I approached what I shall call the "surveillance" or, alternatively, the "discipline and pun-

ish" tent set at the very head of the Benjamin Franklin
Parkway. This tent (of which I shall have more to say
later) was the largest of the Unity Day tents; it was the
first among all competitors of the day's interiors. It was
the Dantesque first darkness, blocking the view (but
not, of course, the sound) of stages from which the music flowed.

The brightness and energy, in combination with the
celebratory rhythm and beat of Unity Day, proved as in-
spirational for me as a "filament of platinum" among al-
loying elements. The beauty, complexity, and expressivity of the Blackness at work on the Unity Day Sunday
afternoon were sufficient to convince even an overly influenced and anxious me that there was a new and important array of energies at work in the world that had
to be accounted for in any story yet to be told of Black
Studies. Like the innovative cultural workers whom I
discovered on the parkway that August afternoon, I realized that I would have to take what I had at hand and,
even under the astute surveillance and policing of the
present day, convert it into a multirhythmic and different story of both academic and general social processes
that have marked the past twenty-five years. I decided
the term *moral panic,* from cultural studies, would nicely
serve my ends. It gestured before and after, as it were,
serving a useful analytical purpose with respect to both
the first arrival of black urban migrants at the gates of
the academy and to the belated current outcry against
that arrival—Political Correctness. Less modishly,
and drawing from the "normal practice" of academic
scholarship, I realized that there was no theoretical or

cultural-studies escape from history. And so the story unfolds.

The new story that unfolds is a drama of shifting horizons, contested spaces, and simulacra. If one recalls the now defunct television show *College Bowl* (which was every thinking man's honorable pastime on Sundays during the early sixties), the image of the American university evoked is a pastoral landscape dotted with spacious buildings, well-dressed white youth smiling and chatting, and studious tweed-jacketed professors earnestly discoursing before rapt audiences. This image of a harmonious garden of knowledge overseen by sober white intellectuals was always shown in brief film clips at half-time for each of the competing *College Bowl* teams matched in rapid-fire responses to "common curriculum" questions of Western Civilization: for example, "What eighteenth-century British economist first announced the iron law of wages?" Usually the participants were young white males displaying a talent for "classical" learning that precious few Americans would ever need to know. *College Bowl*'s pastoral image had become standard fare during the silent American 1950s, and it was not merely a product of smoke-and-mirrors. It carried, in fact, the specific weight of the American academy's founding. For even in the variousness of its founding, the American university was always conceived as a quiet, scenic space of disinterested thought—a territory functionally and strategically removed from everyday life. It is not accidental that seventeenth-century Harvard was called the "seminary in the wilderness."

Without belaboring the point, it seems almost an understatement to say that the American academy is a direct, shaped product of founding ideologies. Sectarian colleges received their marching orders and general character from their respective ministerial governing boards. Private institutions marched to the beat of trustees like Ralph Ellison's Mr. Norton, a manicured obsessive-compulsive from declining New England stock, from the novel *Invisible Man.* The agendas and protocols of state colleges and universities were dictated by legislatures of their home territories. Their life and work were overdetermined by imperatives of the Morrill Acts.

Without ideologies is no American university, to paraphrase Blake, who felt that without "contraries is no progression." Certainly the actual existence and control of American colleges and universities was contrary to their advertised "disinterestedness." John Henry Newman and Matthew Arnold alike knew that it was not disinterestedness that was to be sought in the nineteenth-century British university, but, rather, *escape*—from the messy, modern realignments of race, class, nationality, and knowledge formation that had become far more "public" and "general" by midcentury than either Newman or Arnold cared for.

Until the emergence in mid-twentieth-century America of what Clark Kerr called the "multiversity," United States's campuses were relatively simple and sometimes indisputably pastoral *gardens* of Western knowledge indoctrination, conditioned always by strong and discernible ideologies. With the coming of the multiversity, these ideological interests increased in scale as

big business and big government poured billions of research dollars into the academic garden, transforming it
into a *factory.* What did not change, of course, were the
fundamental whiteness and harmonious Westernness of
higher education. Even when tweed-jacketed white men
were no longer in front of rapt audiences but hermeti-
cally bent on highly financed "research," they were still
white men. Likewise, the student body—even if it was
no longer lolling in tree-shaded gardens—was still, almost to a young man or woman, "white, white, white,"
as they say repetitively for emphasis in most creoles of
the world.

Of course, I am aware that there are exceptions to
this characterization of Western knowledge production.
American universities have always been marked by occa-
sional sites of resistance. And on the whole one would
be hard-pressed to discover the degree of expressive freedom enjoyed by the university in any other American
institution. Moreover, Nathan Huggins has pointed
out in *Afro-American Studies,* a report compiled for the
Ford Foundation, that after World War II, American
universities became more democratic as their enroll-
ments soared, bringing non-middle-class students and
returning GIs to campuses. Catching a general impulse
to reform, universities expanded their mission to include
remedial education and the preparation of traditionally
excluded citizens for upward class mobility. Even with
such changes, however, the exclusivity of America's
well-financed and traditionally all-white sites of higher
learning remained a matter of policy and record. As the
popular philosopher Pogo said in 1963, "Outside pres-

sure [on the American academy] creates an inside pressure: academic conformity. The average [American] professor is no Socrates." Thus, in 1963 the American university was a very quiet, decorous, white project.

My own experiences certainly accord with Pogo's terse depiction of the American academy—I can almost feel, even as I write this sentence, the hushed decorum of the University of California at Los Angeles when I arrived for graduate study in 1965. Eucalyptus and palms shaded wide boulevards and intimate walkways. Quaint outdoor "Gypsy Wagons" supplied orderly dining places for a seemingly endless array of white people. I was thrown into black culture shock by Westwood Village, where even menial jobs were occupied by Mexican Americans, not bodacious brothers and sisters. And when I tried my undergraduate Howard University jive and juju on one of the very few Negro freshmen, greeting him with "What's happening, brother?" he replied, "Why . . . uh . . . good morning. How are you?" His eyes almost bugged from his head in *haute bourgeois* panic. Yes, even though UCLA was indisputably enveloped in the long shadow of the 1965 Watts summer rebellion, the campus maintained a signally quiet grace under national pressure for black liberation. But everything was soon to undergo a change that might have made even Negro freshmen blanch in 1965.

In the midsixties, the quiet of the American university—whether garden or factory—was shattered forever by the thundering "NO" to all prior arrangements of higher education in America issued by the Free Speech

Movement (FSM). Witness those erstwhile docile (or robotic) young white men and women of *College Bowl* transformed into revolutionary cadres questioning the prerogatives of faculty and administrators. Firebrands demanding curriculum revision, deconstructing the rhetoric of American higher education in toto. Witness such rebellion spreading like wildfire across campuses everywhere. What an incongruous moment! Stupefied administrators, faculty, trustees, men and women of the cloth, and bewildered legislators wondered what dread "outside" demon had infected the halls of ivy. For by the midsixties it was obvious to everyone concerned that an outside "social" ambiance and an inside "academic" atmosphere had converged like giant weather fronts. And no one needed a meteorologist to know that a hard rain was gonna fall.

The silencing academic walls were socially breached at midcentury by codes, strategies, and cadences of the black liberation struggle in America. If W. E. B. DuBois speaks persuasively in *The Souls of Black Folk* about a coming of black folk to college that produced new and joyful songs of Talented Tenth enlightenment, surely we can speak today of the emergence on American campuses of strident white students who felt the wind-blown lyrics of a black American liberation spirit moving in their souls. Many of these students had participated in direct nonviolent protests for Civil Rights in their home states; others had made their way to Mississippi during the Freedom Summer of 1964. They were primed for protest, and it is fair to say that the FSM transformed the image of the American university from a *College Bowl* still life into a rollicking video of transgenerational conflict. The country witnessed and responded in deeply condemnatory tones.

The University was transformed, in fact, into a metonym for social chaos. If "mere anarchy" was loosed on America, virtually everyone agreed that the bonds of law and order had been severed by students. "Blame but the students!" became the rallying cry of agreement.

Now the social disorder of the United States was in reality a product of ill-conceived military adventurism in Southeast Asia and a monstrously excessive federal egotism on the home front. The attribution of responsibility for chaos to the university amounted, therefore, to a metaphorical repositioning, a displacement of responsibility that sought to withdraw attention from both American imperialism abroad and vicious United States reactions to black demands for civil rights at home. The voting citizenry of the U.S. decided that it was far more profitable and comforting to scapegoat the university than to assess the criminality of career politicians and their henchmen and constituents at home and abroad.

And it is here that *Black Studies* as a floating signifier becomes a powerful analytical tool. For the convergence of Civil Rights and the FSM did indeed produce incongruity. It was only the further development of this convergence, however, in the form of Black Student Immigration that gave resonance to a revolutionary hybridity on American campuses. For with this immigration, "inside" and "outside" came into brilliant kaleidoscopic allegiance.

Black student recruitment; black student scholarships

and fellowships; black dormitories, student leagues and unions; black faculty recruitment and curriculum revision; and preeminently Black Studies all became signs of new times and territories in the United States academy. *Black Studies* became a sign of conjuncture that not only foregrounded the university as a space of territorial contest, but also metaphorized the contest itself in a way that allowed the sign to serve as a simulacrum. That is to say, *Black Studies* as a sign became not only a *real* ground of contestation, but also a *coded and generative space of values* that encompassed both past and proximate, inside and outside, confrontations. In a word, *Black Studies* became a signifying amalgam of energies gesturing toward antidraft resistance, the FSM, Civil Rights, Black Power, and general American concerns for a redistribution of the resources of knowledge production. In the terms of Jean Baudrillard's *Simulations,* Black Studies was akin to the black box of the genetic code; it was capable of a seemingly endless proliferation of revolutionary "likenesses."

As a simulacrum, *Black Studies* generated a combinatory power of signification in profoundly black ways, mixing styles and producing a synthesis in which kitsch, retro, and other modes occupied spaces of value "all at the same time," to quote Baudrillard on simulacra in general. Before and after, now and future, were temporally coexistent in the Black Studies project, complicating any attempt either to recuperate or authenticate traditional notions of the *real.*

Black Studies was committed in the first instance of its determination to undoing all prevalent "authentic"

notions of such disciplines as history and English.
Hence, at the site of the university, Black Studies pre-
sented a hugely unsettling challenge. For even as it
sought in its own voice to lay claim to disciplinary status as a normal academic subject, its very conjunctive
and stylistically diverse energies eradicated the referential lines of both subjectivity and disciplined academic
knowledge.

How could the notion of traditional disciplines
(bounded as they were by strict codes of nontransgres-
sion) remain unaffected by an avowedly interdisciplinary
view of knowledge production such as Black Studies?
And how—in the face of black immigration—could old
notions of an exclusively white student subject-position
be maintained? Black Studies as simulacrum became the
foregrounded anomaly that arrested "normal" academic
practice and produced both a paradigm shift and the
moral panic and territorial contestation that always ac-
company such shifts.

Thomas Kuhn tells us in *The Structure of Scientific Revo-
lutions* that such shifts are less the result of "discoveries"
than of "anomalies" that can not be accounted for without mind-bending elaborations of old theoretical models
and normal practices. And when there finally is no recourse but to move from a geocentric to a heliocentric
view of the world, watch out! Missiles of panic and conflict are destined to fly.

By 1968, at UCLA, panic was no longer in the eyes
of the young man whom I had greeted with Howard
University argot in his freshman year. Rather, panic was
in the eyes of multiversitycrats witnessing the profound

sea change undergone by this young man between his freshman and junior years. And, Lord have mercy, how *rapid* that change was! By the spring of 1968, that same young Negro who had given me a cool "Hello" was radically hot. He had become a mega-coiffured, dashiki-clad, student leader who audaciously saluted me one morning with "Hey, Brotherman! You gon' be at duh meet'n tonight?" Why even his idiolect had shifted! And it certainly brought panic to the hearts of the nation and produced territorial battles of immense proportions as the young man's fellow blacks migrated to shaded eucalyptus walks of an American university already besieged by the unruliness of FSM and a white countercultural left just awaiting a blackening simulacrum for its dark, revolutionary legitimacy.

In his report to the Ford Foundation, which I have already cited, Nathan Huggins wrote:

> Administrators deliberately set out to recruit poor youngsters from the inner city (so-called ghetto youth), imagining that the university might rectify failures in the secondary-school system and redeem these students so they might enter mainstream life. This policy implied a changing (or at least a rethinking) of standards of admission as they applied to these youngsters.

The recruitment and arrival of ghetto youth on university campuses nationwide was a moment that can only be understood in terms of immigration. Not only did the black arrivants bring radically different racial and

class inflections to the discourse of the academy; they
also brought a hybridity of style that scarcely matched
the "reality" of the American academic garden. Their
very presence on the university landscape challenged all
existing norms and raised citizenship problems that not
even the most imaginative members of the FSM could
have anticipated. Far from "grateful" subjects, the black
arrivants were vociferously cantankerous. Seeing no reflection of themselves at any of the traditional loci of the
academy, they demanded, like Zora Neale Hurston's
Janie Starks, to know, "Where's me? I don't see me?"
This challenging interrogative brought wide-eyed stares
from white fellow students and from faculty and administrators alike. No one had imagined that if blacks were
admitted to the university, they would be anything
other than grateful for such an "opportunity." It was
assumed that blacks, like compliant colonial subjects,
would swear allegiance to Western civilization and
quickly take up the business of assimilating white behav-
ioral codes and intellectual fare. Not so, as Huggins
records: "It was a time . . . of open and symbolic dis-
plays of militancy. Hair styles, clothing, language,
name changes all conspired to challenge and intimidate"
(p. 18). In effect, a new, black academic immigrant culture evolved from the late-sixties through the midseventies. And this evolution was accompanied not only by a
common black discourse across the nation's college and
university campuses, but also by a series of reterritorial-
izations at particular academic locales. Nationally, there
were emergent publications like *The Black Collegian*. Lo-
cally, there were often territorial conflicts between tradi-

tional white inhabitants and a new immigrant population.

In his poem "Old Lem," the late Sterling Brown says: "They don't come by ones . . . They don't come by twos . . . We get the justice in the end . . . And they come by tens." Besieged state politicians and higher education guardians of the early 1970s must have felt that things were rushing at them not by ones or twos, but "by tens." For along with the transgressive black social initiatives that overleapt restraining academic walls in the sixties, there came new revolutionary feminist impulses. Vocal on-campus activism by the courageous Angela Davis and Charlene Hunter was matched by the actions and portraits of such black women social activists as Kathleen Cleaver and Ericka Huggins. At a quotidian level of the liberation struggle, Rosa Parks had by herself begun a fierce war of wills in 1955 when she sat down on a Montgomery, Alabama, bus and decided never to back-off again. *The Feminine Mystique* was being quoted even at Howard University by 1964, and by 1969 even Yale was about to go coed. When women did come to American campuses like Yale, they arrived with the force of tens, and with Women's Liberation on their minds and Women's Studies as their goal. Having failed to listen to any reasonable advice to the contrary, male leaders at Yale decided that what they would do to welcome the coeds and make them happy was paint their rooms in pastel shades and install full-length mirrors. By the fall of 1970, I am happy to report, radical women had seized the mike at a Yale trustees meeting

and demanded the name of the idiot who had prepared
their "welcome." Women's Studies was alive, allied,
and in effect. They came by tens, and they got the justice in the end.

By the 1970s Black Studies had become a point or space
of territorial conflict and conjuncture, containing in its
phrasing both the nominal academic imperative marked
by *studies* and the innovative and surveilling adjectival
imperative *blackness*. Rather than oxymoronic, the tensions in the phrase *Black Studies* signalled an immigrant
hybridity akin to a phrase like *Black British* or *Black
American* uttered in semantic economies that had no
word fields for them. What was required on American
college and university campuses, therefore, was a re-
vocabularization of academic discourse to reflect a genuine redistribution of space, time, and energy to meet
Black Studies demands. What generally occurred, however, in response to the arrival of the new black immigrant population was moral panic as a function of territorial contestation.

In Isaac Julien's brilliant film *Territories,* the word *territory* is defined as "the holding of one's class privileges
in a declining system of crisis." As a "holding," the
dominant territory of Britishness in Julien's film is
locked in struggle with a population that holds quite
other than white British truths to be self-evident. The
film, in fact, projects Black British "Carnival" as a ludic
space of cultural specificity that challenges *all* holdings
of British authority. Voiceovers speak of territories of

17

class, labor, race, and sex relations that have to be oppositionally re-vocabularized and uniquely sounded by a Black British population.

Carnival and West Indian sound systems are portrayed as the ritual and music of Black oppositionality and also as extensions of cultural-expressive forms originating in sacred rites of Africa and the Nile Valley. These sounds and rites of Carnival are captured in Julien's film by swaying masses of Black revellers making their way through the stunned, threatening, or perplexed gaze of massed British police cordons. In one scene a Union Jack's flaming disintegration segues into a shot of two black gay males dancing with each other. The scene surely represents a reordering of territories of patriotism, Britishness, and desire. In a later scene, a pearled and skittish older white British woman hurries along the street until she sees the Carnival revellers; her gaze registers panic. But suddenly the camera reverses, and she moves rapidly backward. The black art of the filmmaker thus challenges the woman's response and returns her to a parochial past from which she may never awaken.

Julien's wonderful mapping of the territories of immigration gives some idea of the stakes involved in Black Studies as black enrollment in American universities mounted to a 10.8% of the total U. S. college enrollment in October of 1977, nearly matching the percentage of blacks in the country's 18-to-24-year-old population as a whole. At Cornell, Wesleyan, and San Francisco State, the new immigration and demands of Black Studies forced confrontations that brought not only panic, but also the police.

As Stanley Cohen defines it in his insightful *Folk Devils and Moral Panics,* a moral panic exists when "a condition, episode, person or group of persons emerges to become defined as a threat to societal values and interests" (p. 9). Characterizing the movement of blacks to the academy, the scholar Nick Aaron Ford writes as follows:

> *Thoughtfully and honestly conceived, and effectively and wisely administered Black Studies are . . . a threat.* They are a threat to blatant ignorance of well-meaning people who are supposed to know the truth about the entire history and culture of their country and its people. They are a threat to prejudice and bigotry nourished by fear of the half-truths and unadulterated lies that miseducation has produced. They are a threat to false and distorted scholarship that has flourished without condemnation or shame in the most prestigious bastions of higher education in this nation. (pp. 188–89)

The threat that produces moral panic results, according to Cohen, in a reactionary sequence of demonizing and surveillance followed by control activities that seek to exorcise the "threat."

Where Black Studies were concerned, the "demonizing" phase witnessed such intriguing figures as John Blassingame, Eugene Genovese, Sir Arthur Lewis, Bayard Rustin, and others delivering exorcising judgments. Blassingame offers a nearly ideal example of

moral panic's attempts to "re-normalize" the
anomalous:

> It is not enough to know that "whitey" has been,
> and is, oppressing blacks. . . . Instead, Negroes
> must study business practices, high finance, labor
> law and practices. . . . the threat to black intellec-
> tuals is real. Not only do the black students de-
> mand that the teachers in black studies programs
> be Negroes, they also want them to have the right
> shade of "blackness." In essence, this means that
> the black scholar must have the right ideological
> leanings.

Blassingame's moral high dudgeon resonates in conservative harmony with the angry tones of President
Richard M. Nixon, whose speech to (and I kid you not!)
General Beadle State College in South Dakota in 1969
called the times "deeply troubled and profoundly unsettled."

The white historian and author of *The Political Econ-
omy of Slavery,* Eugene Genovese, weighed in during
June of 1969, when he portrayed white students as seductive bogeymen leading poor black students down the
road of reactionism. Genovese characterized these leftist
students as "pseudo-revolutionary middle-class totalitari-
ans" intent on coopting Black Studies demands in order
to "reestablish the campus purge and thereby provide a
moral and legal basis for a new wave of McCarthyism"
(p. 108). This is moral panic demonizing with a ven-
geance!

But times of moral panic produce strange bedfellows,

as Sir Arthur Lewis and Kenneth Clark's respective responses to Black Studies demonstrate. Lewis felt the entire Black Studies enterprise was but seedy emotionalism, having nothing to do with the intellectual advancement of black people. Clark, who like Lewis was an academic well-positioned to guide the new initiatives of Black Studies, adopted a posture of complete condemnation. He lambasted the separatist Black Studies program at Antioch College, lamented the failure of the college's administration to stem the tide of what he deemed dogmatism and intimidation, and resigned from the Board of Trustees.

But it would take more than verbal fiats to eradicate the contestatory energies of Black Studies. Thus, the next stage of panic management was launched: policing. At Berkeley and San Francisco State, the California Highway Patrol, the National Guard, and the San Francisco Tactical Squad were mobilized (in the case of Berkeley, under the direct control of then governor Ronald Reagan) to contain the threat. Suddenly American campuses had the appearance of riotous sites of Black British Carnival where settler opposition navigated its way and sounded its unique energies in the very face of the law. Even a police presence, however, could not effect the exorcism. Hence, juridical and all-out political intervention came to bear.

In California, political careers (e.g., that of the late S. I. Hayakawa) were veritably assured by riding roughshod over Black Studies. New demands and tenuous realignments of academic power and privilege were adjudicated out of existence by politics and the courts at San

Francisco State when the entire Black Studies faculty
was ousted in 1974 by then President Hiyakawa. In
other spaces, the outcome of policing was dramatically
different. At Cornell, for example, black students occupied Willard Straight Hall, the student union building,
and took up rifles and shotguns as, at least, symbolic resistance. Cornell's Black Studies arrivants established a
program in 1969 with a $250,000 annual budget and
an aggressively political and avowedly separatist orienta-
tion. In other institutions, Yale, for example, there was
no call for policing because Black Studies was established by students akin to the UCLA freshman. By the
time a militant cadre of inner-city arrivants entered
Yale's gates, the matter had already been settled. Yale's
Black Studies panic was a quiet one.

If moral panics can be read in one light as anxious
moments of policing and control, they can also be read
as boundary crises in which traditionally backgrounded
social problems and actors move to the fore. The American Black Studies moment witnessed a migration of
inner-city blacks to colleges and universities—a movement that disappeared much of the best and brightest
energy of youth from black urban liberation struggles
and placed it under the decorous surveillance of academic administration and policing.

At Yale and elsewhere, however—at Antioch, for instance, with its establishment (to Dr. Clark's utter dis-
may) of a Yellow Springs service station and a black
bookstore as extensions of the Black Studies educational
mission—the sign "community" was never lost. Programs usually contained provisos and funding for "com-

munity" internships and outreach. And the new black academic settler population in or near urban areas always moved between the community and campus. Hence, weekends were made for revolution. Both formally and informally Black Studies forged a connection between everyday black urban life and traditionally dis-interested academic provinces. Here was both a radical reconfiguration and a striking complication of white education in the United States. One might indeed make the stretch and say that after such direct manifestations of "cultural studies in action," how could anyone fail to forecast the birth of more academic programs of cultural studies?

The stronghold established by Black Studies in the American imagination operated not only at local academic sites but nationwide, in such unanticipated spin-offs of the Black History Renaissance, for example, as the late Alex Haley's monumentally successful *Roots*. As the first television miniseries hugely promoted and financed, *Roots* brought Kunta Kinte into every living-room and Kizzy into every kitchen for many nights in a row. An audience of millions watched enthralled as definitions of both *American* and *family* were permanently altered by Haley's *Saga of an American Family*.

Similarly, if there were rooted strongholds that gripped the nation through telecommunal transmission, there were also rock and reggae sitings of Black Diasporic studies. Horns, drums, West Indian sound systems catapulted Bob Marley's *Natty Dread* to international prominence at approximately the same instant as *Roots*. If *Roots* was telepackaged for lightly pedagogical American historical revisionism, Marley's reggae *dread-*

ness was programmed for revolution. Marley, along with other Rasta-inspired artists, brought the Caribbean to us as what the black British scholar Paul Gilroy calls "a diasporic aesthetics" grounded in memories of slavery.

No glitz and glitter and Hollywood high tech—none of this in reggae style. Reggae's motley was an assemblage of old hats, funky dreadlocks, makeshift shirts, uncreased trousers—an absorbing heterogeneity of appearance as Robert Nesta pumped a short burst of Rasta jumps, then seized his head in his left hand and shouted "WE JAH-MING/WE JAH-MING," as an I-and-I sound man. This rough motley of appearance was not a "found" moment, growing spontaneously out of want or deprivation. Rather, it was the dictated uniform of what Orlando Patterson has called "the children of sisyphus"—the followers of the Rastafarian way of anti-Babylonian everydayness. No frills, ornamentation, or material excess shall stand in the way of the coming deliverance from the land of oppression.

Reggae extended Black Studies via the young at already-panicked sites of knowledge production. First, style: the locks appeared. Then, a call for explanation and a threat of revolt: Why do I-and-I inhabit the provinces of *dread?* But not for long. For "If you are the big tree / We are the small axe / Sharpened to cut you down."

The spirituality of Rasta *dreadness* had more domesticated and Christian representations among the black academic settler population in a gospel setting. The Black Church took up residence on campus as the Black Gospel Choir, complete with "young ministers" and entrepreneurially secured robes. As sites of resistance, these "choirs" were like liminal territories of sound—one mind tuned precisely to heaven and the other drawing inspiration from the "church home" in the local "community," which sometimes provided the pianist and even the choir director. Young black Christians were revolutionaries, proclaiming themselves "in no way tired" and offering consolation and strength with their frenzied, sanctified insistence that "God did not bring us this far to leave us."

Here, with the manifold, spatially expansive institutionalizations of Black Studies, was the production out of opposition and contest of an entirely different order of things. Black Studies scholarship grew and prospered, especially in history and literature. And new disciplinary initiatives provided dramatically reterritorialized spaces for black graduate students, faculty, and administrators who had not even dreamed of such academic entry during pre–Black Studies centuries.

If today there are demonstrably fewer programs than, say, in 1973, when two hundred existed in the United States, there is still greater resilience and more abundant scholarly and personnel opportunities than ever before. If funding balances and shifts of ideological allegiances have diminished a *real* black studies, these factors have done little to diminish the spirited force of Black Studies as a simulacrum.

When Black Studies came to the university, its detractors immediately cried up an oppositional force of evil and insidious intent—whether this force was imagined as a black ideological contamination of scholarly

discourse (*pace* Blassingame), a black diminution of standards (à la Clark), or a transgressive militancy. Moral
panics consist in the invention of just such evil forces,
or "Folk Devils." The irony of such invention, however,
is that while it does not properly name the invisible ad-
versary, it is nevertheless correct in its suspicion that a
nontraditional "something not ourselves" is in progress.
The academy's fear that there was more to Black Studies
than met the contemptuously arresting white gaze has
been borne out by the emergence of superb new scholarship, the creation of an immense academic following,
and a tangible redistribution of institutional resources
that could not have been foreseen by those sixties administrators who first opened the academic gates to Black
Studies.

If inner-city youth first brought Black Studies under
the gaze of the American academy, it was always, perhaps, the brilliant black scholar who was proleptically
coded into the "black box" of the enterprise. In 1989
Henry Louis Gates, Jr., wrote as follows: "We are
seeing an increasing number of black studies programs
becoming departments, complete with the right to
award tenure. Over the past 20 years, research methods
in black studies have become increasingly innovative and
'cross-cultural,' responding to the particular nature of
the material and data under analysis by fashioning new
tools." Gates himself is one of the best representations
imaginable of the unanticipated emergence of excellence.
He writes from the "seminary in the wilderness" as a
chaired professor of literary studies and director of Black

Studies at Harvard. He and countless fellow scholars such as Professors Molefi Asante of Temple University and Cornel West of Princeton are joined with innumerable undergraduate and graduate students to build the American Black Studies project securely for the twenty-first century.

This view of Black Studies provides at least some clue to the PC anxieties currently at work in the United States. The late Allan Bloom's influential *The Closing of the American Mind* commences with a sullen and dyspeptic account of the arrival of Black Studies at Cornell. This arrival is described by Bloom in darkly Miltonic terms as Paradise Lost, an expulsion from the academic garden of White Male Philosophical Privilege.

From a Black Studies perspective, the past twenty-five years have been a journey from bare seasons of migration to the flowering of scholarly innovation. From a conservative white male perspective, these same years must have seemed an enduring crisis, each new day and work of Black Studies bringing fresh anxieties of territorial loss.

And if one wonders why PC currents swirl so ferociously about English departments, one need only recall the date September 29, 1968.

On that date, "the trustees of the California State College System voted 85 to 5 to fire one G. M. Murray from his post as an untenured lecturer at San Francisco State College. Murray, a member of the Black Panther Party had been hired as part of an attempt to increase black faculty; he had been teaching courses [as a member of the English department] that were, according to Murray, 'related to revolution.' " (Huggins, *Afro-American Studies,* p. 22)

Many years ago, Matthew Arnold claimed that Western literary cultural capital—poetry in particular—might be the sole currency that human beings had left to invest in an age of mechanical reproduction and the untimely death of God. But the notion of preserving infinite historical value and unquestioned excellence in the referential files of the English department is at best a quixotic extension of Arnoldian cultural economics. For reliant as it is upon the fundamentally human power of the "word," "naming," "nommo," the site of English is always subject to unexpectedly defamiliarizing change.

Certainly, the rhythms of black urbanity brought to campus by Black Studies unsettled the quiet Western reserve of English through the revolutionary intentionality of figures such as Murray as well as the dazzling scholarly moves of an emergent Black Studies criticism and theory that quickly gained international prominence. The PC controversy swirls madly about English because it is the site that has been most dramatically altered—in axiology and method—by the energies of Black Studies. Hence, the heavy dramas of policing English through histrionic purges such as that of Murray, or through ludicrously hyperbolical jeremiads like those of the PC Cavaliers should come as expected returns of the always repressed. So much of the present PC orchestration reduces, I think, to the latest pas de deux between black urbanity and English values begun during the sixties.

Finally, my own concluding return is to Philadelphia's Unity Day and the gargantuan surveillance tent at the top of the Benjamin Franklin Parkway during the summer of 1991. The tent was itself a kind of new simulacrum. In its yellow and white exterior gaiety, it seemed the perfect complement to Unity Day, a shaded place of conviviality, an updated version of the revival space that past black generations spiritually inhabited, a place of picnic rather than panic.

But once inside, what wonders did unfold. Around the tent's inner perimeter were display tables manned by uniformed men crisp in their appearance and concentrated in their attention to duty. Here were Philadelphia policemen, Pennsylvania Highway patrolmen, Drug Enforcement Agency officers, U. S. Army Counterinsurgency troopers, and United States Department of the Interior rangers—among others. The purpose of the tent—placed at the head of the Parkway—was the recruitment of young, black, urban men and women to the precincts of American "discipline and punishment." From the perspective of the tent's official personnel, it was possible to maintain surveillance over all of the assembled and predominantly black sharers of Unity Day. The complications of inside/outside were more intricate, though (as you might well imagine), than the officer's inner point of view.

Along one rim of the tent's interior, there was also a battery of card tables equipped with chess boards where pairs of black youngsters were serenely ignoring the recruiting officers and playing the Western board game of war with dread equanimity and deft, black style. As the music of "Rasta Timothy" and a variety of young, black male and female rap groups flooded the tent, the black youngsters at the chess boards moved with the rhythm, playing rapidly and slapping the timers with stunning low fives. No one, as far as I could detect, was interested in heading for the recruiters.

I think I truly startled, surprised, and then seemed a great opportunity to the United States Department of the Interior ranger to whom I said "Hello" after wandering away from the dynamic chess players. He saw me looking at the leaflets on his table and said: "Do you know Edgar Allan Poe, sir?"

Well, there it was! English reclaimed for purposes of police recruitment in the public sphere of surveillance. If even the devil can quote scripture, it would seem that even the police can find use value for English in the extraordinarily dynamic black youth sphere of a new public culture.

The idea driving the Interior Department's Poe moment (which was emblazoned by an 8×10 sheet containing a silhouette of the author) was that the nineteenth-century American writer's biographer had given a false view of Edgar Allan as a drug user. The ranger corps was convinced that Poe had, in fact, followed the example of Nancy Reagan's model citizen by just saying "No."

The policing and administering of a transgressive Poe by the official surveillance tent for purposes of recruitment, was not, I thought, very different from the discipline-and-punish frenzy of the new PC offensive. For like the Department of the Interior rangers, the PC

Edgar Allan Poe

National Historic Site
Philadelphia

National Park Service
U.S. Department of the Interior

Did Poe Just Say No?

Edgar Allan Poe's creepy horror tales, adventures and beau-
tiful poems are world famous.
Poe could string the right
words together to make your
spine tingle, excite you or make
you feel things deeply. But he
also has a reputation for having
been strung out on drugs.

Why?

How The Confusion Began

Poe loved being a writer. He
thought that he knew the best
way to do it and he tried to tell
everyone else how they should
write their stories, too. So,
other writers, their feelings
hurt, became very angry at
Poe. When he died, one of
them began making up bad
things to say and write about
him. Poe wasn't there to tell his
side. Soon, others began
believing these things even
though they weren't true. They
even said that Poe used drugs
to get ideas for his stories and
poems. How did Poe really get
his ideas? He got them by
reading many books, maga-
zines and newspapers; watching how people behaved; and
using his wonderful imagination. Then he chose words
very, very carefully to make his
stories and poems exciting and
believable.

Say No To Drugs

Have you ever tried to write a
story or rhyme? If so, you
know that it can be very hard to
pick out just the right word to
say exactly what you mean. It
can be impossible if you don't
feel well or are thinking of
something else. If drugs take
over people's lives, people
stop caring about their home-
work, friends, family and future.
They just think of getting more
drugs. There is no room for
anything else like writing stories. Poe was talented and
hard working. You are talented, too! Poe did not need
drugs and neither do you. Let
your imagination fly free. Don't
depend on drugs.

Say no to drugs!

Edgar Allan Poe Emblazoning. Courtesy Edgar Allan Poe National
Historic Site, National Park Service, United States Department of
the Interior.

Cavaliers seek to contain the energies of all arrivants at the territories of knowledge production by recruiting them to a ludicrously "cleaned up" version of the Western past. Of course, what was so intriguing about the drama playing itself out on Philadelphia's Unity Day was the rhythmic motion of the black players who had the surveillance tent itself well under control and conditioned by a steady urban beat.

That beat has carried Black Studies from academic immigrancy to forceful, scholarly citizenship in the American university. And the new story of Black Studies is the amazing proliferation of its energies in a manner that makes avoidance or eradication impossible. This proliferation will not be contained through the massive doles of panic-stricken foundations, nor by the commencement rhetoric of American chief executives. Today, and in future, the best that resisters and anxious crisis managers can hope for is rhythmic coexistence. This is both the immemorially old revelation—more nourishing than bread and more stimulating than new wine—and the stunningly new story of Black Studies in these United States. As Public Enemy might make the point: "It's like that y'all!"

2

THE BLACK URBAN BEAT: RAP AND THE LAW

The black urban beat goes on and on and on in the nineties. The beat continues to provide sometimes stunning territorial confrontations between black urban expressivity and white law-and-order. The summer of 1992 furor over Ice-T's powerful creation "Cop Killer" was only the latest instance of rappers v. the law. N.W.A. (Niggaz With Attitude), a group based in Compton, produced the spectacular album *Straight Outta Compton* several years ago, and gave an impetus to "gangster rap" and anti-establishment expressivity that has scarcely been matched. The album's most controversial cut was "F . . . the Police!" a creation that motivated a letter from the FBI to N.W.A.'s record company. By the time of the Los Angeles insurrection in the spring of 1992, it became obvious even to the television news anchors and talk show hosts that rappers like Ice-T, N.W.A., and Ice Cube (an original member of N.W.A. who has gone solo) had been prophetic with respect to tensions between black urban

youth and metropolitan police authorities. It was precisely the type of jury-exonerated violence against the
black Rodney King that urban rap had in mind when
it claimed that police justice was but another name for
young-black-male victimization. And the fiery violence
of the spring of 1992 in Los Angeles was just the kind
of "armed response" that N.W.A. had prophesied in
its versions of the strength of "street knowledge" recorded on *Straight Outta Compton.*

Now the investigation of confrontational instances between rap and the law carries Black Studies well beyond
the limiting boundaries of any single discipline, for such
territorial conflicts often demand an improvisational flex-
ibility and a historicizing of form that are not always
characteristic of academic responses to popular cultural
forms.

Thinking of one form of American law that has been
nationally summoned by no less a citizen than the recent black Supreme Court appointee, we recall vivid
lines from the oeuvre of Sterling Brown:

It wasn't about no woman
    It wasn't about no rape . . .
They strung him up on Main Street
    On a tree in the Court House Square
And people came from miles around
    To enjoy a holiday there.
They hung him and they shot him,
    They piled packing cases around,
They burnt up Will's black body,
    Cause he shot a white man down;

'He was a man, an we'll lay him down.'
("He Was A Man," *Opportunity* June 1932, p. 179)

Brown's stanza makes the point that black men are con-
victed—indeed, *X-ed* by lynch law—under the sign of
sexuality. The true reason for their legal *X-ing,* however, as the stanza also makes clear, is the justified fear
on the part of white men that a black OG (Original
Gangster) order does exist, and that in such an OG
imaginary, someone is always desirous of actually shooting the sheriff—or at least of challenging seriously the
law on its own public and economic grounds.

We meditate the legal "X" of erasure—not in an
effort to assume the role of latter-day phenomenolo-
gists—but to consider the inversive and brilliant powers
of symbolic transformation possessed by African Americans. The "X" of white-motivated legal erasure and
"unnaming" is recuperated as black re-nominalization.
"X" becomes the ground zero of a virtual nation striv-
ing to "make it real." Ralph Ellison defines the process

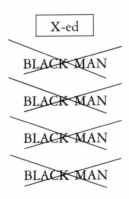

as creating music from invisibility. The Nation of Islam writes it as the initial refiguration of a specifically white American misnaming of Africa. In the 1990s, young black urban men and women literally put their heads into the "X." Those X-caps, which casual observers deem mere fashion statements or simple metonyms for Malcolm, are signifiers of a national blackness oppositionally testifying against American legal obscenities like the spring 1992 acquittals in Simi Valley.

If the academy has served as one "inside" space of confrontation between black urban transformative energies and the law in recent decades, surely a vibrant "outside" site of confrontation in our immediate past has been the urban park. If the inside moment of Black Studies was preeminently a matter of contested visions of the world, then recent park events were indisputably matters of audition—a contestatory sonics, as it were, of attempted white *X-ing* and its bodacious black resistance. Events unfolded as a legal *hearing* on and in the park.

The *New York Times* for 21 April 1989 read: "A young woman, jogging on her usual nighttime path in Central Park, was raped, severely beaten and left unconscious and bloodied in an attack by as many as 12 youths, who roamed the park in a vicious spree Wednesday night, the police said." The "Central Park Jogger" panic had begun. The "young woman" was a Wellesley and Yale graduate, Phi Beta Kappa, Salomon Brothers investment banker boasting an academic record that had never been lower than "A —". Her work at Salomon was heralded as "top notch." She became the object of shrines in the

park, vigils, and a special mass that *Newsweek* for 8 May
1989 reported as follows: "At the weekend she was near
death, her brain severely damaged from two skull frac-
tures. Five hundred of her co-workers attended a special
mass at a church near Wall Street. But in the grim
neighborhoods north of the park, youngsters showed little sympathy for the beaten woman. 'She had nothing to
guard herself, she didn't have no man with her, she
didn't have no Mace,' a 12-year-old told New York
Newsday." (Having commenced this section, I am
drawn away from its sharp, analytical pull to record the
horror—abject, absolute, beyond any frame of reason—
the *horror* of what actually happened to the young
woman. What Salman Rushdie might call "Actually Existing Brutality" took her as its April sacrifice. Nothing
about the young woman *in herself* demands from reasonable human beings a response other than deep compas-
sion. The tragedy of the young woman's brutalization,
however, was that she was seized again after-the-fact,
and used *for others*.)

The park became the significant space of an unfolding
panic. Not, mind you, the park *tout court,* but what the
Times story of 21 April called: "the northern reaches of
the 840-acre park. That area has not yet seen the vast rehabilitation that has touched many other sections of the
park in recent years."

Could it be that rehabilitation north of 90th Street
was delayed due to that sector's proximity to grim northern neighborhoods uptown? Are we really speaking here
of East Harlem at the 102d Street Transverse where the
investment banker was attacked or not? Yes, we are

speaking of East Harlem. We are speaking, as well, of media and public-sentiment construction of a poetics of space that is less significant or sacred for the *presence* of the park than it is remarkable for the *absence* of Wall Street. (The recurrent media maps showing the 102d Street Transverse might well have been drawn on the parodic scale of the *New Yorker* cover, known to all, which depicts Manhattan as the dominant and consuming territory of a caricatured map of the United States.)

We cannot discount *Central Park* as a metonym for the brutalization of public spaces. But, as in 1929, the actual *panic* was on Wall Street—that great American site of controlling interests and regulations that police the boundaries between public and private property. And, no, it is not as simple as "class warfare" between the Salomon Brothers set and savagely rebellious East Harlem teenagers of color. It is both more and less than that. What, after all, is Central Park?

Purchased in 1856 for in excess of 5-million dollars, the park was laid out by the landscape architect Frederick Law Olmsted. On its original committee of overseers were such stable citizens as William Cullen Bryant, Washington Irving, and George Bancroft. Without rehearsing the history, mythology, and iconography of the park, it is surely not an overstatement to say that its vast, green acres were meant to provide memorial, recreational, and "natural" spaces of display within the rich, industrial, and financial embrace of the metropole. A green, aesthetic space of purposive purposelessness—with, in fact, the *very purpose* of showing precisely how industrial/financial purpose could pay off for those who truly understood the American gospel of wealth.

Olmsted was introduced early in life to what he later described as the power of "scenery." His father loved nothing more than long, contemplative rides through "domestic" scenery like that found on English estates. Such arranged scenes of gardening represented, according to the boy's father, the results of cultivated taste. Their effect upon observers was, in a word, *civilizing*. This early fatherly point of view was reflected in Olmsted's own notion of the desirable character for Central Park.

The park was to be a republican institution insofar as it scenically extended the civilizing effects of genteel tastes to an entire urban citizenry. It was to be, as it were, greenery with a mission. Olmstead felt that New York, with its burgeoning immigrant population, was equivalent to a frontier in need of civilizing influences such as his envisioned park. He wrote: "We have nowhere on the western frontier a population newer to its locality and so little socially rooted or in which it is possible for a man to live so isolatedly from humanizing influences and with such constant practice of heart-hardening and taste smothering habits as that to be found in our great Eastern cities."

Central Park, then, was to become a hugely constructed greensward excluding the sights and sounds of New York. It was to be an architectural simulacrum of instructive nature. The project utilized thousands of men, tens of thousands of purchased trees and shrubs, countless man-hours, and millions in actual dollars

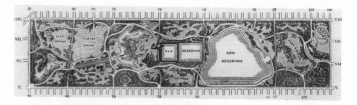

Plan of Central Park (*top*) and Detail of Drawing "No. 9. From Point I" from the Olmsted and Vaux presentation of the Greens-ward Plan, Frederick Law Olmsted Papers. Courtesy Municipal Archives, Department of Records and Information Services, City of New York.

drawn with byzantine political wrangling from the coffers of New York.

In addition to his plan to "wall" out the city from the park, Olmsted was keen on sufficient policing to insure that the "ordinances of the [Park's] Board are respected and obeyed" (p. 80). Further, he and Calvert Vaux, coauthor with Olmsted of the winning design for Central Park, were aware that the park required sunken transverse roads for the passage of traffic—not only to avoid the presence of such traffic in the park, but also to ensure the nocturnal passage of traffic: "The transverse roads will also have to be kept open, while the park proper will be useless for any good purpose after dusk; for experience has shown that even in London, with its admirable police arrangements, the public cannot be secured safe transit through large open spaces of ground after nightfall" (p. 121).

Central Park, then, is public space controlled, in purpose and finance, by enormous wealth; public space utilized and overseen, at its best, by well-connected private citizens such as Bryant and Irving who represent the type of genteel cultivation of taste that Olmsted wished to mirror. (There are, of course, too many stories about park accessibility for me to spend much time on the point. But simply call to mind the scene in *The Long Walk Home,* when Whoopi thinks she can have a Chicago kind of "Saturday, in the park," thinking it is the Fourth of July. The police quickly remove her. Also, if you will, indulge me in a moment of recall: I will think back to a segregated, "colored" Chickasaw Park in Louisville, Kentucky. What a bitter irony it was to have segregated parks in Louisville—most of them for whites only—named after American Indian nations. And how perverse of Louisville's city fathers to name the "colored" park after the only Indian nation that submitted itself to servitude.)

If Central Park represents public space, then surely most of both the park's "public" and its "space" are held in a type of private trust—save, to be sure, the "northern reaches." An offense in, or against, or counter "the park" is held to be a blow to "our city," a rank violation of "public" space. But offenses in, against, or counter the welfare, safety, and life of "public" schools, "public" housing, or "public" welfare are held to be proof of the ethnic or class worthlessness of private individuals dependent upon such resources.

In a word, only the "public" that is traversed, utilized, staged, or displayed for the benefit of those who have some indivisible interest in the doings of Wall Street can serve politically, emotionally, or aesthetically as the site of urban offense. Space such as Central Park that has been constituted as "valorized" public space is, then, a geography rife with symbolic potential. It is both "natural" and urban, a ludic playground and a territory of fierce control, a combination of democratic vistas and explicitly policed zones of exclusion.

But even before the symbolic potential of Central Park erupted in the national media in April of 1989, at a temperature that could have melted titanium (melting point $1,675°C$), the contestation of urban public spaces was already launched in a way that only acquired new intensity in the wake of April 19th. For which of us did not engage in at least one knock-down-drag-out debate with a friend or relative some seven or eight years ago about the public-space ethics of the "boom box"— sometimes unflatteringly called the "ghetto blaster"?

When young America (especially young, black, urban America) began to set up acoustical shop with gigantic, multi-decibel-capacity radios and tape decks—began to set up shop in American public spaces (buses, street corners, sidewalks, and, of course, parks)—the hue and cry, lamentation and gnashing of polemical teeth threatened to deafen us all. Why couldn't these young people—especially the "ethnic" ones—wear headphones?

Or just die? What made "them" think "we" wanted to be infected with their—well, you really couldn't call it MUSIC, could you?—with their *noise?*

The argument about boom boxes was not only a John Stuart Millian quibble over the nature of liberty with respect to silence and noise. It was equally a panicked response by some citizens to what they perceived as the ethnic pollution of public space by the sonic "other." In part, the argument was a generational matter, and the young, who are always irreverently inventive and cleverly reductive, simply shouted: "If it's too loud, you're too old!" More than generational, however, the contest was urbanely proprietorial: Who *owns* the public spaces? What constitutes information and what constitutes noise? Just what is visually and audibly pure and what precisely is noise pollution or graffiti? The more the conservative older folks condemned, the larger the boom boxes grew. The greater the proliferation of ordinances against it, the more rampant became the spaces of graffiti. In 1992 the disruptive sound of black urban youth is mobile, a jeep beat produced by gigantic speakers specially installed in the rear of 4×4 vehicles—whatever the owner-DJ can afford to drive.

Urban public spaces of the late twentieth century are spaces of audiovisual contest. It's something like this: "My billboards and neon and handbills and high-decibel-level television advertising are *purely* for the public good. Your boom boxes and graffiti are evil pollutants. Erase them, shut them down!" No wonder the black rap group has to call itself Public Enemy (PE) when it aggressively enjoins an audience to "Bring the

Noise!" The orchestration used by PE's producer, Hank Schocklee, has been referred to as the "wall of noise" technique. The "public" and its "enemy" are joined by PE in a spatial imaginary of silence and sound, urbane and primitive, civil and tribal.

The Central Park jogger incident was continuously set before media consumers as a question. If the causes for the savage attack on the investment banker in Central Park did not include drugs, alcohol, poverty, class, or racial motives, then what answer could be given as the reason(s) for the attack? "Why? Why? Why?" The media dunned sociologists, psychologists, teachers, social workers, teenage interviewees. The explanations were all, it seemed, unsatisfactory, and no one could provide a sufficient "why."

The reason the Central Park jogger incident yielded no credible "whys" was precisely because the incident itself was *the answer*. It was the answer to the question that could have been formulated anytime during the past decade by almost anyone over the age of thirteen and breathing—the answer to the question: "What will happen next in the great contestation marking northeastern American urban, public spaces?" It is surely ex post facto, Monday-morning quarterbacking to make this claim and to say that Central Park was predictable as a site for the moral panic of April 1989. But, after all, it *is* Monday, and the game has played itself out, leaving abundant video, audio, and print traces for ex post facto analysis. Is there ever any other kind of analysis?

New York City chief of detectives Robert Colangelo

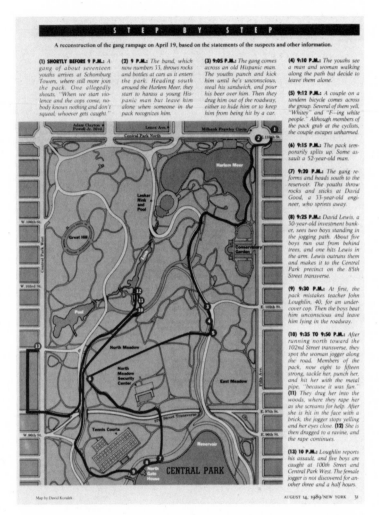

Reconstruction of April 19, 1989, Gang Rampage in Central Park.
Copyright © 1992 by K-III Magazine Corporation. All rights reserved. Reprinted with permission from *New York* magazine. Map by David Koralek.

said: "the attack appeared unrelated to money, race, drugs, or alcohol" (*New York Times,* April 22, 1989, p. 1) and went on to say that some of the more than thirty or forty youths involved in a general rampage through the park "told investigators that the crime spree was the product of a pastime called 'wilding.'" Colangelo admits: "It's not a term we [the police] had heard before."

Wilding. How ominously uncivil and antipublic it sounds! Yet how commensurate with the site of its invention. Wasn't the idea of the park as urban public space precisely to preserve some frisson of "the wild" for citizens with Wall Street connections? Further, don't the very "natural" configurations of the park as civil space suggest a controlled "wildness"? Isn't the place of the zoo—a caged and culturally constructed "wildness"—in the park?

But, of course, the framers of the park don't really mean it, do they? I mean aren't they like rich evangelists—even the semihonest ones—who preach damnation fiercely to an unruly flock. Like Satan, however, these evangelists are always surprised by sin! So, too, are those who socially construct an exclusive wilderness for urban display. They are caught entirely off guard when their errand—any errand they choose—in the wilderness, a wilderness which they grasp only as a simulacrum, is met by the *wild.* The well-connected are wilderness simulators. The consequence of their wild surprise is panic par excellence.

The irony of Central Park, East Harlem, and Wall Street is that the jogger panic revolved so much around hearing, around the auditory aspects of public spaces. We have already re-invoked the specter of the boom box. But what about the transformations of parks into sounding spaces of rap music during the 1970s? The park was a favored locale for hooking up a sound system to a lamp post—draining off public power, as it were, to fuel the music of Public Enemy—and providing the driving, rhyming, dissing, and dismissing sonics for a "jam" against the ennui of, say, "grim neighborhoods."

But by 1989 these early park sonics had become not simply a boom-box annoyance to well-connected walkers in the city, but a rappers delight for the international marketplace. The contest between Wall Street connectedness and unrehabilitated isolation in the northern reaches of the park had, thus, been somewhat levelled by the abundant capital suddenly available to young black men as a function of the innovative sound they had created both in and for international public spaces.

Where is *wilding* in all of this?

Well, those who followed the jogger-panic know what bizarre assumptions and conclusions can result from white public *hearings*. (We had our fill of such bizarreness in the U.S. Senate hearings during the fall of 1991, didn't we?) For if Detective Colangelo had never heard of *wilding,* neither had the audience sampled by Barry Michael Cooper, who recorded the following in his essay for the special *Village Voice* issue (May 9, 1989) devoted to "The Central Park Rape":

> The strange thing is, the kids I talked to uptown in El Barrio—kids who listen to the rap shows of

DJ's Red Alert and Marley Marl, the supreme arbiters of new-jack-speak—said there's no such word as "wilding." When I asked many of them about it, they laughed at me, looked at me as if I was on the pipe. "Wilding?" one asked me with his eyebrow cocked. "I ain't never heard of that. Sounds like a white-boy rock type of thing." Kareem from Tres Unidos said, "I've heard some people say, 'Yo, I'm going to do the wild thing,' like the Tone-Lōc song, which could mean a guy going to have sex with his girl, or just having a good time. Since we as blacks and Puerto Ricans tend to slur our words when we use slang, somebody probably said that to a white reporter, and since that person probably didn't understand what was said to him or her, they clarified it by inventing the word 'wilding.' But I had never heard of it, until I saw it in the headlines."

The sonic connection that Colangelo and other New Yorkers were missing comes, as it turns out, by way of Los Angeles and the rapper Anthony Smith, who began his adult entrepreneurship by buying California houses, renovating them, and reselling them at a profit. Smith's nom-de-stage became Tone-Lōc (pronounced with a long "o") when his voice was discovered and marketed by two young white businessmen named Mike Ross and Matt Dike. Ross and Dike knew the techniques of and had a passion for rap. What they lacked was a representative voice; they found that voice in Tony Smith. Sampling Van Halen for a guitar riff, they took the phrase "wild thing" from Fab Five Freddy and Spike Lee. (See *Rolling Stone,* June 1, 1989, p. 31). Then they contracted Young MC (an LA-based rapper) to write lyrics. They put the resultant mix at the disposal of Smith's raspy voice. Lo and behold! A mega-hit called "Wild Thing" was born! Tone-Lōc became a contender.

The Wall Street aspect of this collage of youthful energies—this West Coast bricolage—is the fact that "Wild Thing" quickly became the second-best-selling single since 1985's "We Are the World." The follow-up success of Lōc and company's "Funky Cold Medina" (also written by Young MC) helped the album *Lōc-ed after Dark* become the first album by a black rapper to hit number one on the pop charts.

In a column for *Commentary* (March 1990), Terry Teachout observes: "Every New Yorker who reads the papers knows that the teenagers who allegedly raped and brutalized a woman jogger in Central Park last year entertained themselves after their arrest by collectively chanting the lyrics to 'Wild Thing,' a popular record by the Los Angeles rapper Tone-Lōc" (p. 60). Well, everyone may have known this nearly a year after the event, but in April of 1989 there was only a mishearing rife with significances that we have yet fully to decode in 1991. The chief of detectives and others heard not "wild thing," but "wilding." They thus became hermeneuts of park panic, connecting such phrases as "roving bands" and "wolf pack" to a cultural phenomenon for which they held no adequate public hearing. Suddenly every self-righteous entrepreneur of panic, every self-proclaimed moralist of the public order was pronouncing on *wilding* as though he or she were the authority for the encyclopedia entry for the term. Tipper Gore and Susan Baker speak out on *wilding* in *Newsweek* for May 29, 1989. *Time* does its wild thing in the May 8 issue. By January 13, 1990, Andrew Stein, president of the New York City Council, can enjoin:

> *The police should begin to gather intelligence on wilding attacks, identify the schools and subways where they are most likely to occur, and beef up their presence there.* School officials should be encouraged to warn all students that if they are caught, the authorities will try to send them to jail. (*New York Times*, January 13, 1990; italics added)

Now, I would claim that rap economics, in contest with the public law and the law of the "public," had more to do with the writing of the Central Park jogger incident as a moral panic of "wilding" than anything else. We might ask, for example, if the offense committed in April 1989 was so rare that it comprised a wholly new form of brutality against women?

In *The Nation* for May 29, 1989, we are reminded that in 1987, in the wake of an incident of sexual harassment and a "Take Back the Night" march, a wolf pack of thirty-five white Princeton University men roved the campus chanting, "We can rape anyone we want." The *Nation* article also reminds us that "Middle-class men viewing *The Accused* have cheered the film's harrowing rape scene (p. 1). Professor Peggy Sanday of the University of Pennsylvania has written of male brutality toward women on college campuses as the norm in her pioneering study titled *Fraternity Gang-Rape,* which begins with a violent incident at the University of Pennsylvania.

Both the form of victimization and the gendered "attitude" of the victimizers in the Central Park jogger case were completely known and horrifyingly resonant in America. What distinguishes the "wilding" panic of Central Park from other instances of sexual assault is surely its status as the response to an auditory and fiscal competition between young urban blacks who would profitably "bring the noise" and urbane civil Wall Street generations who do not want "banking" limits extended to northern reaches of the park.

Finally, it was *Newsweek* that flung off the mask of bafflement, bracketed the ceaseless "whys," and went moralistically straight for the jugular of new black male urban energies. The cover of the magazine's March 19 issue reads:

RAP RAGE
Yo! Street rhyme has gone big time
But are those sounds out of bounds?

The forehead and big eyes peeking over half-lowered sunglasses on the cover belong to none other than Tone-Lōc. Within weeks, George Will conflated the Central Park jogger incident, "wilding," and rap music with (who else?) 2 Live Crew. Lo the return of the repressed! Here is Will:

When arrested a defendant said, "It was something to do. It was fun." Where can you get the idea that sexual violence against women is fun? From

a music store, through Walkman earphones, from
boom boxes blaring forth the rap lyrics of 2 Live
Crew.

Obviously Will is not like "every" reader of New York
dailies since he seems to have no knowledge of Tone-Lōc
and "Wild Thing," which his home magazine had just
indicted. But what is most remarkable about Will is
not his moralizing belatedness, but his Wall Street pro-
tectionism. The key lines in his column seem to be the
following, which appear under the subheading "No
Morals":

> In such selling [of sounds morally offensive, to
> George Will] liberals are tools of entertainment cor-
> porations. The liberals and the corporations have
> the morals of the marketplace.

Will thus seems to want only *specific,* Wall Street corporate interests to be represented and protected in public
spaces. "Liberals" and "corporations" would seem, in
Will's account, to be an amoral combination willing to
carry boom box soundings into the public sphere where
they result in criminal, black, male outlawry.

Finally, I think Will is not protesting obscene lyrics
and their gender consequences at all. Rather, I think he
is concerned to police the flow of capital for cultural production in general. (Certainly, this is not a concern unknown to us in the wake of Pat Buchanan's successful
assault upon the National Endowment for the Arts and
George Bush's less-than-heroic dismissal of that organiza-

tion's leadership.) With his talk of corporate interests, doesn't Will realize that Luther Campbell and 2 Live Crew are *independents* who have their own precisely non-Wall-Street sound? I believe that at some deeply subconscious legal level George Will does realize the independence of Luther Campbell and company. I further believe that it is just this independence that compels the Washington columnist to construct a pseudocommunist corporate bogeyman to account for the international success, inventiveness, and basic black entrepreneurship that puts rap in the park—that locates Tone-Lōc and 2 Live Crew successfully outside the law, challenging Wall Street dominance and prime-time American media to a public showdown. The economics read something like the following from *Rolling Stone,* August 9, 1990:

> He [Luther Campbell] owns a Jaguar, a BMW convertible, a Westwind jet and a new home. Campbell won't disclose his net worth, but one magazine estimated his assets at 11 million last year.

We montage now to the primal scene of Judge José Gonzales of Florida ruling Luther Campbell and *As Nasty as They Wanna Be* obscene, leading the way for the sheriff of Broward County to arrest two members of the crew in June of 1990.

By June 9, John Leland, music critic for *Newsday,* has already announced that the Crew's cultural production is a matter of a quite specific code of black-on-black creative signification. Leland suggests that the code is easily available as black public knowledge, if

Luther Campbell of 2 Live Crew. Photograph courtesy Luke
Records.

Tone-Lōc. Photograph courtesy Delicious Vinyl, Inc.

only the law would take time to listen. Economies of Wall Street and the park on trial in Florida—this is postmodern allusive positionality par excellence.

By June 19, Henry Louis Gates, Jr., echoes Leland and reinforces defense strategies set in motion by Bruce Rugow, lawyer for the 2 Live Crew. Gates goes Leland one better—not only is the Crew's sound representative of a code of black public knowledge, but their presentational strategies are, according to Gates, "part of a venerable Western tradition." Their work is not only parody, but also, I assume, analogous to Western art. A literally breathtaking judgment! Certainly, the judgment takes one's breath away if one considers the overall mediocrity (by the standards of, say, EPMD, PE, or Eric B & Rakim) of the Crew's production. In arriving at this opinion, Gates offers the following justification in an op ed essay for the *New York Times* on June 19, 1990:

> 2 Live Crew is engaged in heavy-handed parody, turning the stereotypes of black and white American culture on their heads. These young artists are acting out, to lively dance music, a parodic exaggeration of the age-old stereotypes of the oversexed black female and male. Their exuberant use of hyperbole (phantasmagoric sexual organs, for example) undermines—for anyone fluent in black cultural codes—a too literal-minded hearing of the lyrics.

Gates goes on to discuss the group's evocation of the carnivalesque and the signifying practices of black culture in general. His argument is intended as a culturally specific account of 2 Live Crew's sound as expressive art. His apologia for the Crew, however, seems an example of the black man of words' hyperbole. As Richard Wright is reported to have said to a particularly favorable reviewer: "Man, you went way beyond the book!" Gates goes a good way beyond the actual production of the 2 Live Crew.

We all know the story's ending. Luther and 2 Live Crew are acquitted. The young white foreman of the six-member jury says the jury acquitted the brothers because they were funny (O, shadows of darkest minstrelsy!). As the *New York Times* for October 21, 1990, reported: "Jurors said they did not agree with the defense's assertion that the 2 Live Crew's music had to be understood in the context of black culture. They said they thought race had nothing to do with it" (p. 30). Again, this is breathtaking! In this instance, however, one is left breathless by the arrogant refusal of attention to the specifically black character of rap as a form.

The whole of the law's machinery was brought to bear in Florida, and against 2 Live Crew. I see this, in an ironic way, as a postmodern consequence of surfaces and allusions. For surely the Florida lawyer Jack Thompson, who alerted the sheriff about the Crew, became a guardian of Central Park purity and Wall Street connectedness in the 2 Live case. The *New York Times* for October 17, 1990, reports:

> In recent weeks, [after the 2 Live Crew arrests had taken place], Mr. Thompson has also begun pro-

testing the music of two new rap groups, Geto Boys and Too Short. He runs his campaign from his two-bedroom home in Coral Gables. With the help of a compact disc player, he transcribes song lyrics he finds obscene. He then sends them by facsimile machine to record companies, reporters, law-enforcement officials and politicians.

CD players and fax machines come to have as much to do with the machinery of the law and the policing of the park as the thirty new officers who were added to the Central Park force in the wake of the "wilding" panic.

There can be little doubt that the order of things—especially the law—was the scene of a major shift between April 1989 and the acquittal of 2 Live Crew in October of 1990. The shift was a function of a new hearing of public spaces and a rewriting of the park via Wall Street and rap.

The hope now, I think, is that the rewriting, or better the *resounding,* of the law will produce a larger public concern than simply the contested geographies of the park can provide. It would be salutary, for example, if the "grim neighborhoods" of public housing were to reap the benefits of the type of hearing provided by the Central Park moment. Then perhaps we would not only see the horror of that black woman who was forced to a Brooklyn rooftop, raped, and murdered in the same time frame as the Central Park jogger assault, a rape and murder that were very much unreported; we might also find in our new public concern both exacting and effective ways to channel the transnational capital of everyday rap into a spirited refiguration of black urban territories—a refiguration that would foreclose even the possibility of such horrendous black woman victimization as that in Brooklyn, and a refiguration that certainly would prevent the veritable silencing of such obscenity.

It is not incidental that we call to mind at this point the energy that John Singleton's film *Boyz in the Hood* acquires at the very moment that its athletic hero is gratuitously murdered. The moment of Ricky's death represents an epic erasure of black youth energy! What is the media response to Ricky's death? Doughboy, Ricky's rapping and inversive half-brother played by the rapper Ice Cube, tells us that he has watched *all* of the news and there wasn't "shit" reported about his brother. Doughboy's conclusion: "Either they [prime time media] don't know, don't show, or don't care about what goes on in the hood."

Positive sites of rap represent, I think, a profitable, agential resource for an alternative American legality. At such sites as the "Stop the Violence Movement" and HEAL (The Human Education against Lies rap coalition) black men and women "bring the noise" about the white law's silencing. Both coalitions of rappers began in recent years and showcased the positive energies of such stars as KRS-One, Kool Moe Dee, Heavy D, Flavor Flav, Just Ice, Chuck D, and others. These positive sites of rap are as energetically productive as those manned by our most celebrated black critics and award winning writers.

Finally, we must hope that the shift in the order of things effected by the park events of recent years will be analytically articulated by present-day Black Studies. For where Black Studies, rap, and the law are concerned, there exist myriad interconnections and scholarly opportunities. Where and how we choose to site ourselves with respect to the public space of Century 21—where we choose, as it were, "to park"—is far more an option with respect to Black Studies than it has ever been in the history of the American academy. Surely the time is now for Black Studies scholars to continue the work begun in the 1960s of rewriting (and righting) the law.

It was, of course, Blake who taught us that "one law for the ox and the lion is tyranny." We have broken such tyranny in our era precisely by re-sounding and multiplying the inflections of the law, refusing to allow any statute whatsoever to restrict our access to the dynamics of, shall we say, "parking" in America?

3

EXPERT WITNESSES AND THE CASE OF RAP

apping the force of black urban expressivity in its relationship to American law-and-order is, at least, a multivocal Black Studies enterprise. It demands committed familiarity with historical variables and sonic registers of popular cultural forms as they actually exist in the world. It is scarcely enough simply to say that rap, for example, is a black male expressive form bearing some nonce-formulated relationship to a general "black art." Nor is it enough simply to label rap a new, noisy mode of urban resistance that paradoxically appeals both to middle-class white youth and the black underclass. The complexity of rap's relationship to a Black Studies investigation of "outside" signifying events such as the Central Park jogger incident and the LA Insurrection seems so resonantly important that it puts in bold and almost ludicrous relief a general American ignorance of the form. I believe this ignorance is a willed refusal fully to engage a form that is preeminently young, black, and male.

Unlike rock and roll, rap can not be hastily and pro-
lifically appropriated or "covered" by white artists. For
the black urbanity of the form seems to demand not
only a style most readily accessible to black urban youngsters, but also a representational black urban *authenticity*
of performance. There are successful white rappers, to be
sure, but they are but tiny hatches on the great totemic
structures of the form. Likewise, there are successful
black women rappers, but proportionally they represent
a cluster of stars in a vast constellation. Two indispensable aspects of the form—its blackness and its youthful
maleness—seem to occasion a refusal of general, serious,
nuanced recognition.

The paradox of this refusal, however, is an unwitting
complicity in the form's influence and spread. For example, many Americans—young and old, black and
white—will "hiply" boast of their children's (or some
child's, perhaps a cousin's or a nephew's) familiarity
with rap. They will even share schmoozing anecdotes
about corporate or religiously inversive occasions of rap
usage to which they have been party. Few, however,
will study or acknowledge the sites and history of rap's
black male productivity or the brilliance of its resonant
inner-city inventiveness and strategies of resistance.

We thus witness such pitiable instances of ignorance
as a white or black parent adoringly watching her two-
year-old gyrate to *Sesame Street*'s alphabet rap while assur-
ing a telephone interlocutor from next door that she
hates rap because it is a woman-bashing, uninventive ca-
cophony of local black noise for the lower classes. Such
arrogant ignorance is not only pitiable, but also costly

in economies of global understanding required for a coming century. Rap's global appeal was chronicled by the
New York Times for August 23, 1992. In a long report
compiled by a number of writers, the significance of the
form for Russia, Japan, England, France, Mexico, the
Ivory Coast, and elsewhere is explored. The conclusion
seems to be that rap is one of the most important shap-
ers of popular styles globally.

Certainly, in the voluble instance of Central Park and
the legal hearing to which it gave rise, rap refused to be
ignored. It not only produced a striking legal and expressive cultural intertextuality in black and white acoustical spaces, but also an unexpected scholarly witnessing
that seems seriously to compromise the best effects of
Black Studies. I want especially to reflect on the process
of academic "expert witnessing" occasioned by rap and
the "outside" park events already discussed.

In Stanley Kubrick's film *Full Metal Jacket,* there is a
high postmodernist moment in which a Vietnamese prostitute weaves her way through Saigon traffic in order to
solicit two American GIs seated at a sidewalk cafe. Surrounding the threesome are the gears, levers, and confusion of a frantic metropolis. The prostitute rubs herself
sensually and says: "Me so horny. Me so horny. Me love
you long time." The rest of the scene plays as a reaction
to the cultural imperialism of war. It ends when the GIs
are robbed by an angry Vietnamese boy who flees with
his partner on a jazzy motorscooter.

Watching the slick moves of one of Arsenio Hall's
New Jack nocturnes during the spring of 1990, I suddenly felt hauntings of the already heard when the host

intoned: " 'Me so horny. Me love you long time.' Wow! How about that 2 Live Crew!" It turned out, of course, that 2 Live Crew had sampled (appropriated phrasing from) Kubrick's movie to enliven what was to become the most popular rap song on the group's album *As Nasty as They Wanna Be.* The rest of the story is history. As I have already detailed, the album was the first in the United States to be banned by a federal judge; members of the group were arrested after a live performance in Florida, and the controversy surrounding the Crew became all the rage in 1990. The group had its day in court and won, due in large measure to the testimony of expert witnesses employed by their lawyer.

The best-known witness for the defense, as I have already acknowledged, was Henry Louis Gates, Jr. Gates's testimony at the trial in Florida continued his earlier line of apologetics. It was his opinion that the Crew was funny, was possessed of "great virtuosity," and was a signifying site of black, artistic, cultural transmission.

Of course, 2 Live Crew's vicious sexism had been remarked by Gates in his op ed essay, but his prescription for this deeply negative aspect of *As Nasty as They Wanna Be* was to "look toward the emergence of more female rappers to redress sexual stereotypes." Critical responsibility for black cultural capital seems tragically lacking in this prescription. Furthermore, to promote the violent nastiness of 2 Live Crew as achieved "genius" is a serious disservice to the best traditions of rap itself. The music of 2 Live Crew is in no way beyond the average mix. And their rhyming abilities and delivery skills rank only in the very middle range of rap performance.

For a respected Afro-American literary critic to exalt and justify the sexist mediocrity of *As Nasty as They Wanna Be* is seriously to relinquish agential responsibility. It is also, I believe, an indication that Gates's "witness" was not motivated by even a reasonable standard of comparison. It seems highly unlikely to me that if Gates had been fully informed about and invested in the dynamics of rap as a popular cultural form he would have made such extravagant claims for 2 Live Crew.

One of the latest discursive installments on the history of expert witnessing set in motion by Gates occurred in the December 1991 issue of the *Boston Review,* which carried two essays devoted to rap and to the 2 Live Crew respectively. The first essay by Professor Kimberle Crenshaw, who teaches law at the University of California at Los Angeles, is titled "Beyond Racism and Misogyny: Black Feminism and 2 Live Crew." The second, written by Mark Zanger, who is identified as a "veteran Boston journalist," is titled "The Intelligent Forty-Year-Old's Guide to Rap Music." Crenshaw's essay is a direct response to the 2 Live Crew history. Zanger's is harder to characterize, existing midway between pseudoacademic pastiche and scholarly burlesque. Crenshaw's stance on rap is captured by her statement, "The debate over 2 Live Crew illustrates how race and gender politics continue to marginalize Black women, rendering us virtually voiceless. Black feminism endeavors to respond to this silencing by constructing a political identity for Black women that will facilitate a simultaneous struggle against racism and patriarchy" (p. 33).

The duality marked by "racism" and "patriarchy," according to Crenshaw, constructs a zone of "intersectionality" in which Black women are relegated to subordinate status. As an "intersectional" spokesperson, Crenshaw first mounts a jurisprudential defense of *As Nasty as They Wanna Be,* arguing against the album's banning for obscenity, and claiming that 2 Live Crew's creativity does not serve prurient interests and is not devoid of artistic value. In fact, Crenshaw argues that the banning of *As Nasty as They Wanna Be* was a function of white American racism; it was a judgment intended to eradicate the palpable threat of the Crew's black male lyrics to the chastity of white womanhood.

Accepting at least the spirit of an artistic defense of *As Nasty as They Wanna Be,* Crenshaw next moves to a more black womanist plane, offering a sharp critique of Professor Henry Louis Gates, Jr., for his defense (as an expert witness in the trial) of 2 Live Crew, a defense based precisely on the group's black artistry. Crenshaw seems to suggest here, in a truly curious about-face, that just because the Crew's album is black "art" and enjoyed by a black audience does not mean that such creativity should be condoned, accepted, or circulated as black art by the black community.

Now surely, there is at least confusion in this critique. I believe this confusion has its root in the founding binarism of Crenshaw's case for "intersectionality" in general. For she asserts binaries all too facilely, I think, between race and gender, black men and black women, intersections and what I would call materialist disjunctures, art and everyday life.

Guided by such porous binaries, Crenshaw seeks in her public essay to present a cultural nationalist tableau of an Afro-American subculture replete with sui generis forms of art, forms that must not be ignored or minimized by the white world, and that certainly must not be banned as obscene. 2 Live Crew thus receives a spirited *Miller v. California* defense against obscenity from Crenshaw the black academic who derives cultural capital and self-advantage at the site of the university from a nationalist ontology. But what the academic hand giveth, the black womanist hand taketh categorically away.

For it would seem that Crenshaw, given her critique of Gates's position, does not wish to categorize *As Nasty as They Wanna Be,* in any traditional sense that I can infer, as black community art essential to the transmission of valued, conventional modes of life-enhancing behavior. Instead, as a black womanist she views 2 Live Crew's efforts as violent expressions of patriarchy. This Janus-like logic does not augur well for the utility of intersectionality, nor does it substantially increase our knowledge of the cultural intersections of rap in the economies of American law or in the cultural politics of Black Studies. Now, here is Zanger, and I quote:

> Rap's main poetic forms are long lyrics and dramatic monologues, with interesting revivals of choral poetry and dialogues. Didactic poems and satires fill out a basically eighteenth century formal

portfolio. Hit raps tend to be more repetitive, like short Romantic lyrics. Attempts at longer forms, such as rap operas and concept albums, haven't succeeded. We're a long way from a rap epic. Slick Rick, a fine storeyteller, seems to hold a one-rapper niche as a balladeer. (p. 9)

This is an example of the pseudoacademic pastiche to which I earlier referred. It marks one pole of a binarism not terribly unlike Crenshaw's category of art. For in Zanger's argument, there is also a downside to rap that seems to draw fire. This negative pole for Zanger is the adolescent dumbness or stupidity of rap. And, finally, the veteran journalist seems less interested in an academic artistic defense of rap based on English prosody than in an almost strangely middle-aged voyeurism before what he constructs as the adolescent sensibility—sexual and otherwise—of rap. Ignoring the heavy politics and cultural nationalism of groups such as Run DMC and Public Enemy, Zanger provides an "Aw, shucks, Ma, they're just children" mapping of rap economies.

What the accounts of Gates, Crenshaw, and Zanger reflect, I believe, is a form of expert witnessing that deflects serious attention from the complexities of popular Afro-American expressive cultural studies. Their accounts also represent, I'm afraid, a drearily conventional mode of response by adult scholars to popular cultural forms. This traditional adult scholarly response is what I call the "start in the middle of the game" approach. Let me explain.

A media-reported controversy or a dinner party conversation or a tragic public event (such as the Central Park jogger episode) occurs and calls attention to one or to an array of popular cultural forms. I think most grown-ups (if at all possible) ignore the popular cultural form, the controversy, the public event, and everything else beyond the walls of their home. If the adults are academics, they will tell you their obliviousness is a function of too many committees or of studious residence in the long dark tunnel of the tenure process. They will insist that they never have time to raise their heads above the level of iambic pentameter or the middle style of publishable prose.

However, if the triggering event that brings a popular cultural form to attention will not go away, or if it is taken up by media networks that seem to work in only two modalities these days—"wedge" issues and "infotainment"—then even the most oblivious adults seem compelled to write something (to write *anything*) or to take action vis-à-vis the popular cultural form in question. Gates's trial witnessing and the essays in the *Boston Review* seem to demonstrate the typology I have in mind.

As far as I can deduce from the *Boston Review,* it was the emergence of the 2 Live Crew that motivated Crenshaw to pay serious scholarly attention to rap. However, popular cultural forms, as scholars such as Andrew Ross, Nelson George, Greg Tate, bell hooks, Cornel West, Tricia Rose, and others have pointed out, are always amazingly freighted with historical and cross-generational weight. Popular cultural forms remind me, in

fact, of such functional and materially inscribed imple-
ments as sculpted West African measuring weights.
These artifacts can be literally worth their weight in
gold and yet uncannily determinative in everyday forms
of cultural exchange. They may be rife with historical
(and aesthetic) importance and yet functionally foregrounded in the everyday life of a society. They create
spaces where people determine relationships among competing values and myriad possibilities. In a word, these
measuring weights bear dense and multiple cultural
freight.

Why, then, in the presence of the specific densities of
rap, would Crenshaw adopt intersectionality as an analytical construct? For her claim, if I have understood and
discussed it properly, is that if you are of a mixed consti-
tution—such as black *and* woman—your life is more difficult and your manner of thinking about things more
complicated than if you are simply black or simply
woman. We have seen, I think, the confusion that results from such binarism. And it is, finally, a binarism
that relies heavily upon essentialist assumptions difficult
to credit in our age. For we inhabit an era in which
any of us might encounter (simply in our daily travels) a
black, Vietnamese-American, potential-MBA, Ivy-
League, basketball-playing woman who is fully at ease
with the transnational, material, and indisputably hybrid spaces in which she dwells. Hence, Crenshaw's intersectional thinking seems to offer a somewhat belated
problematic as we face contemporary multiplicities. It
seems, in fact, a case of special pleading. When one ex-
plores the life and oratory of such historical figures as

Sojourner Truth and Harriet Tubman, one encounters black women who had no trouble whatsoever posing the query "Ain't I a woman?" in ways that made the simple one-liner an eruptive, voluminous declaration of black women's liberation—and a veritable encyclopedia for cultural studies—not unlike the African measuring weight.

So what is the special efficaciousness of Crenshaw's intersectionality in legal discourse, or in the current history surrounding rap? How does it differ, for example, from the carnivalesque as defined by African American griotic tradition, which has traditionally been occupied by men as well as women? How does it differ from the spaces of the voodoo priestess, who, in one very real sense, is never at an "intersection," but always at the perceptual and imaginative beginnings and endings of all roads that lead everywhere? The voodoo priestess mediates pathways between heaven and earth, ritualizes the marriage of heaven and hell, life and death.

Applying Crenshaw's intersectionality to the 2 Live Crew—or, at least, applying it in the dualistic manner suggested by its author—is rather, I suspect, like deciding whether one is going to vote for George Bush as a man or woman, or as a *whiteperson.* That is to say, by any standard that I can envision, 2 Live Crew is bafflingly controversial for one reason only: media networks and "instant experts" have made them so. I am not suggesting, of course, that 2 Live Crew's productions in themselves are innocuous. But I do believe that the controversial might be reserved in this day and age for things that are unusual. And there is certainly nothing unusual about the persecution, arrest, and prosecution of black men within a psychosocial frame-up of sexuality in America. So why do we need to make choices about whether 2 Live Crew's misogynistic, violent, juvenile lyrics directed precisely against humanity (conceived, idealistically, as people who would live together in harmony) should be condemned?

I suppose the argument for the defense rests largely upon the plea, "But, officer, the cars in front of me were speeding too!" Of course, the prosecution would intervene here with the facts, saying 2 Live Crew's album *As Nasty as They Wanna Be* was the first record to be ruled criminally obscene by a federal judge. But the defense would grow even more agitated before such facts and point out that in the United States there is a penchant for antiwomanism, misogyny, pornography, incest, and wife battering among the male population of late-twentieth-century life. Male brutality, to invoke the caveats of *Miller v. California,* is the "community standard." Still, in the voice of the prosecution, one might suggest that the widespread existence of male sexual brutality does not mean that any given appearance of it should be regarded by *scholars* as simply another speeding vehicle on the highway of popular culture's dark underbelly. (Although we might easily instance the 2 Live Crew, as I have done in my foregoing discussion of Central Park, as mightily successful entrepreneurial "outlaws." Their sonic capitalism is a remarkable counter to Wall Street controls. The *remarkable,* however, is not necessarily the *commendable.*)

So, if 2 Live Crew can not be defended on the grounds that "others do it, so why persecute we?" then why would a scholar defend them on precisely such grounds? The only motive that leaps to mind is a kind of essentialist loyalty to blackness or "the race," that is, the cultural-nationalist self-advantage already mentioned.

The more abstract argument, as I understand it at a general plane of expressive-freedom discourse, is that although we may not like a particular form or brand of speech, still the First Amendment and our postenlightenment humanitarianism compel us to defend such speech to the death. This form of endorsed voluntarism seems altogether noble, but it also, in the 2 Live Crew instance, seems more vaguely charitable than I am willing to be.

I want to be very clear and explicit here. My argument is that the speech and behavior of 2 Live Crew should not be endorsed on any grounds other than purely fiduciary ones (a kind of outlawed sonic capital resistance) in a world where we hope to move toward more humane standards of behavior. My point of view is harmonious, I think, with antipornography advocates like Andrea Dworkin and Catharine MacKinnon.

I believe 2 Live Crew's album was understandably banned. And I believe that if women and minorities were empowered to assume genuine agency in American society, other such albums would probably be banned, along with Andrew Dice Clay, *Hustler*, *Penthouse*, and peep shows. Though social scientists and policy analysts are fearful of declaring a correlation between the volume of violent, obscene, antiwoman drivel available in the United States and the incidence of violence against women, common sense alone suggests such a correlation. And social constructivists must be hardpressed to make a large case against such a correlation. For who does not know that pornography is a multimillion dollar criminality, organized and controlled by men who genuinely are as nasty as they wanna be?

I am certainly *not* suggesting that the criminal prosecution of popular artists should become a United States norm. Nor am I advocating the institution of a kind of State PC (in this instance, "popular culture") police force to roam the land instituting "standard" words and works in lieu of popular idioms. What I wish to emphasize, as I have earlier implied, is that popular cultural forms are historically weighted, contemporarily useful, and *always* extraordinarily various. To refuse to recommend, listen to, or endorse the 2 Live Crew is, in no way, to make a general or simplistic judgment about rap music. For, in ways that I hope I have made clear, 2 Live Crew is less a causal site of agency than a single point of imbrication in an intricate social (and preeminently materialist) narrative.

In the creative and ever-expanding world of rap, there are works firmly dedicated to women's rights. There are efforts devoted to the eradication of violence from the black community (e.g., the Stop the Violence Movement, which I have already mentioned). There are raps that make the strongest case (and perhaps the *only* case available) to young urban blacks against child abuse and acquaintance rape. There are raps designed to teach black children their own specific history. There are raps that decode (and perhaps they are the only sources among certain young black people that do so) the relationships of policing and surveillance to the rights of individuals in a "free" society. There are raps that send instructions to young black men on how to "be a father to your child."

To privilege, therefore, and foreground in expository prose (using some of the most interesting minds of a generation) the 2 Live Crew is like spending a significant portion of one's life thinking about George Bush as a fit and admirable model of a visionary and imaginative politician. If one concentrates on what I call positive sites of rap and sets these sites in the context of the video imaging that one samples on BET (Black Entertainment Television) and MTV, then one realizes how signally creative, important, and varied rap is as a generational form—perhaps as the last relay and ultimate outpost of teenage redemption in an aging United States. Answer me this: What good middle-class homeowner would think immediately of defending Free Enterprise upon returning to her home and finding that somebody had made off with all her stuff? And who among us, with common sense, is going to spend her best energies seeking to weave a defensive First Amendment blanket for adult males of color who decide they can "bank" all the "dead presidents" they wish by being as nasty as they wanna be? Such a defense, it seems to me, clearly manifests only the presence of what the rap ensemble HEAL (Human Education Against Lies) calls *CSDS*— Common Sense Deficiency Syndrome. HEAL—

comprised of Big Daddy Kane, LL Cool J, MC Lyte, Queen Latifah, KRS-One, Run DMC, and others— would be outraged at such a defense.

If you set out purposely to contest the law, to offend the standard, to insult and repulse the public, then how can you yell "foul" when the law slaps you? Yes, you can demand the separate-but-equal condemnation of George Carlin or Eddie Murphy in order to fashion yourself as an enlistee in a history of popular resistance to reactionary codes of decency and standardization. Still, in pointing to the prevalence of pornographic magazines, comedians, movies, videos, and even topless donut shops (yes, there was one such shop in Broward County), your implied remedy would have to be more akin to Kurtz's injunction in *Heart of Darkness* than to a vaguely messianic query about individual persecution. Your line would not be "Whyfore persecuteth thou me?" but "Exterminate them all!"

But since it is popular music and our agency in relation to it that is the focus here, let me say that I believe Tipper Gore *is* a puritanical busybody who should not be listened to by anyone under the age of 135. And I think the Parents' Music Resource Center should be locked up (for a very long time) in an elevator playing a continuous loop of the history, politics, sociology, and music of popular culture.

Nevertheless, it would be not only hypocritical but quite stupid of me to suggest that black people must like and accept everything that comes under the sobriquet of any particular black popular cultural form. Though strict constructionists of the Western canons of "art" will deny it, there is a very great deal of banal junk included in the named archives of the West's *greatest hits* category. Which person among us believes that every Mozart or Beethoven is beyond the touch of the trite and banal? Who has journeyed in any of the world's museums without wondering: "Why in the heck did they hang this piece of junk . . . even if it is a 'Picasso'?"

Which is only to say that no named formal archive is one hundred percent *even* with respect to greatness and purity of achievement. Every tradition is rife with, as it were, space junk that upon close interrogation comes floating down like lead out of the reifying heights of impressionistic critical puffery. Why should the archives of rap be held to a different standard?

To uncritically endorse all of rap's moments would surely support the notion of a blind obliviousness to a historical tradition in which blacks have been continuously oppressed and bothered by a dominant culture telling them that the songs that *must* have meaning for them are "Happy Getting Up in the Morning" songs. We all remember the scene in *Uncle Tom's Cabin* when Simon Legree suggests to his recently purchased black bondspeople that he doesn't want to hear any old lugubrious melodies from a population he is carrying into hell. Legree shouts: "Shut up, you black cuss! . . . did ye think I wanted any o' yer infernal old methodism? I say, tune up, now, something real rowdy,—quickly!" I know that there is in the world of popular culture, as it is perpetuated in an atmosphere aggressively tolerant of pornography, no discounting audience taste or control in product formation and dissemination. Like Legree, I would not set my sights on an old methodism, for religion or for scholarly critique.

By citing positive, informational, imagistically vibrant rap sites of black-youth knowledge formation, I am not gesturing toward some utopian "innocent sexuality" to set against a libidinous 2 Live Crew. (Something "really rowdy" is always the supplement, isn't it, of even our most innocent desires?) By "innocent," here I mean not only "puppy love," but also *non-over-determined* by market conditions. (Witness the controversy and instant editing that greeted Michael Jackson's "rowdy" crotchrubbing, widowsmashing primetime premiere for *Dangerous.* Even an androgynous Michael was not innocent enough before an American audience to get away with such stuff.) We can perhaps end this line of reflection, then, simply by saying that when *I* was asked to appear as an expert witness for the defense on behalf of a record shop owner in Canada who was being brought before the law for selling 2 Live Crew's album, I refused to go.

The reason I refused to go might be economically stated in the single word *agency.* Black Studies enables us to realize that in an age of transnational trading zones, the familiar delimited and delimiting apparatus of the nation state—including laws, amendments, policing, and morality—are no longer as simply identifiable as during earlier moments with Marx. That is to say, I would not consider myself solely in league with the state if I adamantly refused to commend or defend *As*

Nasty as They Wanna Be. (Although in the instance of this particular album mine and the state's impulses might well coincide. And, of course, I am in agreement with the state's quite mysterious decision to allow me to retain a handsome job in one of its preeminent sites of knowledge production.) Rather, I would think of myself as a scholarly, even a Black Studies, site of discriminating agency with respect to community popular cultural interests. Aware of the trading zone proliferation and diffuse agency occasioned by today's global, speed-of-light transfers of capital, I reserve, with Black Studies equanimity, the possibility of a selective black agency despite the new Legrees of Wall Street, Tokyo, and Berlin.

Perhaps we can now sample a somewhat different tack, one coextensive with the reservations with which I began, about scholars who start in the middle of the game and witness themselves as "experts." Recall with me for a moment one of the most magnificently misanthropic lines in English literature, when Dickens's most famous miser asks: "What! Are there no poor houses?" When one reads Gates, Crenshaw, and Zanger, one queries: "What, are there no books on rap? Are there no magazines and informative television shows?" One asks these questions because the writers mentioned appear to have felt no compulsion whatsoever to interrogate the complexities of the zones of the "popular" to which they pretend expertise. They were not motivated to come up to speed on rap as an expressive cultural form. I happen to know of the following interesting and easily accessible books that deal with rap: *Cut and Mix; Signifying Rappers; Nation Conscious Rap; Bring the Noise;* and *The Rap Attack.*

In addition to these books, scores of more topical and glossier sources exist. There is, moreover, a full journalistic history and accounting surrounding rap as a form. MTV and BET, as I have earlier suggested, offer practically nightly examples and commentary. Rap, these resources make clear, is scarcely a phenomenon that sprang from nothingness.

As the musicologist and cultural critic Paul Gilroy has so comprehensively shown in *There Ain't No Black in the Union Jack,* an African disasporic aesthetics does exist and must be taken into account in all matters of black social analysis. Rap has a contemporary function in such an aesthetics. But we don't need even a hint of Afrocentrism to verify the statement that rap is not a totally recent emergent or "instant" form susceptible to expert witnessing as I have here defined it. The most rudimentary scholarly effort shows that the form traces its history from the late 1960s.

Where is this history of form—this cultural, material, and historical weightiness—in the writings of Gates, Crenshaw, and Zanger? I don't want to be too uncharitable to the *Boston Review* posse; the scholarly life has its demands. But unfortunately, one such demand (or seduction) seems to be the demand for instant experts who exposit virtually at will about popular cultural forms. "But," you say, "isn't such instantaneous commentary precisely why the forms that are its object are 'popular'?" And the answer is, "No," in thunder. To say whatever you will about emergent popular cultural forms simply because you are an adult scholar and feel that nobody will challenge you since your colleagues are too busy deciding which Chardonnay to serve at the next dinner party, is as bogus, sloppy, and irresponsible as you wanna be.

Yet the demand felt by forty-something experts seems to be to get "hip" and provide instant-replay analysis in the fashion of commentators for Monday night football. However, the instant-replay mode vis-à-vis historically situated and resonantly important forms of transnational cultural expressiveness constitutes only a self-aggrandizing act of scholarly hipsterism. It is, one might say, a totally self-interested form of popular hucksterism.

It won't do, of course, to say to our instant experts, "You ought to be perfectly ashamed of yourself!" But one might recommend that they be at least as exacting in their knowledge of rap as the rappers they pretend to discuss, defend, categorize, or witness for. Since I am clearly over forty and approaching the big five-o, however, I probably stand no more chance of being trusted by a younger generation than anyone else who claims to be an adult expert.

Still, I believe that Black Studies have bequeathed, especially to black scholars comfortably situated in the contemporary academy, a proud legacy of brilliant territorial gains. To compromise such a legacy with academic hucksterism and instant-expert witnessing for national and transnational media networks is, by any standard that I can envision, a signal betrayal of the bridge by which present-day black scholars "got over." What precisely is it that motivates such a betrayal? In part I think it is the allure of name recognition; if one signs on, no matter how ill-informed he or she may be, at the proper sites of black solo production, then a mass audience may come to associate only the soloist's name with the entirety of, say, the Black Studies enterprise. To recognize the name is to acknowledge, in this scenario, an "expert."

But such foolish closed-loop credibility manufactured by transnational media networks is precisely what Black Studies was designed to eradicate. Black experience and urban signification were intent on de-legitimizing and relegating to the junkyard of white history the old saw for scholarly certification that reads, "I got my job through the *New York Times!*"

Beyond name recognition and its entailments, there is a new politics of desire at work in the world today that leads formerly resistant black scholars to cry out for the healing blessings of neoconservative opinion makers, foundations, bards, and reviewers. We witness case studies in which the most surprising sources tell us that one scholar or another has "come around" or "backed off" or "seen the error of his earlier extremism."

I am, of course, paraphrasing from conversational memory here, but the general spirit of the critique is that many who held up their hands and were chosen as adherents for the Black Studies project have now decided to sit on their hands and urge the lowering of the signifying hands of former allies. Alas, it is as though many of the field workers for Black Studies have been just too undone by the seductive politics of the Big House!

Finally, there are money and careerism as causes of betrayal that need no further elaboration by me; surely there has been, as the rappers say, *'nuff said* about all of that, y'all.

In what seems to be a time of desirous, willing, and treacherous "expert witnessing," to call for a new, or at least a retelling of the story of Black Studies in its relationship to black urban culture seems a necessary act. The relationship of both projects to the law should be enough to make any sober-minded Black Studies beneficiary in today's academy somewhat hesitant about the allures of instant expertism. For surely under the aegis of such expertism one relinquishes analytical force, axiological clarity, and pedagogical presence. The black urban siting of Black Studies demands not instant experts glibly pronouncing on the relationship between popular and black urban cultural forms. Rather, this siting and the expressive cultural resonances to which it gives rise —the complex intertextuality that it occasions and the hard axiological choices vis-à-vis, say, the state that it compels—demand the same type of historical, ethnographic, and intellectual perspicaciousness required to comprehend the African measuring weight. The "popularity" of a form does not automatically imply that it is "simple." And simply because both the form and you are black does not mean—T-shirt mottos notwithstanding—that you automatically understand.

How then does the Black Studies scholar "inside" the

academy productively sound the territories of rap and analyze its "outside" energies in meaningful ways? First, one has to attempt stylistically and historically to move in harmony with the form's own displacements. Next, I believe, one needs to theorize the form's resonances in terms of—to quote KRS-One—"Where you are and what you do." "Inside" and "outside" might thus converge in strategic forms of instructional resistance for the future. I want now to extend my reflections on black urbanity and the academy by attempting just such a sounding of form.

4

HYBRIDITY, RAP, AND PEDAGOGY FOR THE 1990s: A BLACK STUDIES SOUNDING OF FORM

Turntables in the park displace the machine in the garden. Postindustrial, hyperurban, black American sound puts asunder that which machines have joined together and dances to hip-hop acoustics of Kool DJ Herc. "Excuse me, Sir, but we're about to do a thang—over in the park and, like how much would you charge us to plug into your electricity?" A B-Boy, camp, site is, thus, established. And Herc goes to work—with two turntables and a truckload of pizzazz. He takes fetishized, commodified discs of sound and creates—through a trained ear and deft hands— a sound that virtually commands (like Queen Latifah) assembled listeners to dance.

It was the "monstrous" sound system of Kool DJ Herc which dominated hip hop in its formative days. Herc came from Kingston, Jamaica, in 1967, when the toasting or DJ style of his own country was still fairly new. Giant speaker boxes were essential in the competitive world of Jamaican

> sound systems . . . and Herc murdered the Bronx
> opposition with his volume and shattering fre-
> quency range. (David Toop, *The Rap Attack*)

It was Herc who saw possibilities of mixing his own for-
mulas through remixing prerecorded sound. His enemy
was a dully constructed, other-side-of-town discomania
that made South and West Bronx hip hoppers ill. Disco
was not *dope* in the eyes, ears, and agile bodies of black
Bronx teenagers—and Queens and Brooklyn felt the
same.

LeBaron Taylor was the entrepreneur who moved to
create a crossover moment in which black R & B stations would be used as testing grounds for singles
headed for largely white audiences. Johnnie Taylor's
1975 "Disco Lady" was one of the first hits to be so marketed; 2.5 million singles sold. And the rest is history.
What was displaced by disco, ultimately, was R & B, a
funky black music as general "popular" entertainment.
Also displaced (just *dissed*) were a number of black male
classical R & B artists. Hey, some resentment of disco
culture and a reassertion of black manhood rights (rites)
was a natural thing. And what the early hip-hoppers
saw was that the task for the break between general
"popular" and being "black by popular demand," had
to be occupied. And as Albert Murray, that longtime
stomper of the blues who knows all about omni-
Americans, put it: In the *break* you have to be nimble,
or not at all! Queens, Brooklyn, and the Bronx decided
to "B," to breakdance, to hip-hop to rhythms of a dis-
membered, sampled, and remixed sound meant for ener-

getic audiences—in parks, in school auditoriums, at high school dances, on the corner (if you had the power from a light post—and a crowd). And Herc was there before Grandmaster Flash and Afrika Bambaataa. And hip-hop was doing it as in-group, urban style, as music disseminated on cassette tapes—until Sylvia Robinson realized its "popular" general possibilities and sugared it up at Sugarhill Productions. Sylvia released "Rapper's Delight" (1979) with her own son on the cut making noises like "to the hip hop, hippedy hop/ You don't stop . . ." The release of "Rapper's Delight" began the recommercialization of B-ing. The stylistic credo and cryptography of hip-hop were pared away to a reproducible sound called "rap." And "rap" was definitely a mass market product after "Rapper's Delight" achieved a stunning commercial success. "B-style" came in from the cold. No longer was it—as crossover/commercial—"too black, too strong" for the popular charts. (But, of course, things have gotten stranger and 2 Live since then!)

So, rap is like a rich stock garnered from the sudden simmering of titanic B-boy/B-girl energies. Such energies were diffused over black cityscapes. They were open-ended in moves, shoes, hats, and sounds brought to any breaking competition. Jazzy Jay reports:

> We'd find these beats, these heavy percussive beats, that would drive the hip hop people on the dance floor to breakdance. A lot of times it would be a two-second spot, a drum beat, a drum break,

and we'd mix that back and forth, extend it, make
it 20 minutes long. If you weren't in the hip hop
industry or around it, you wouldn't ever have
heard a lot of these records.

Twenty minutes of competitive sound meant holding
the mike not only to "B," but also to set the beat—to
beat out the competition with the "defness" of your
style. So—it was always a *throwdown:* a self-tailored,
self-tutored, and newly cued game stolen from the multi-
national marketplace. B-style competed always for (what
else?) consumers. The more paying listeners or dancers
you had for circulating cassettes or ear-shattering parties
in the park, the more the quality of your sneakers im-
proved. The idea was for youth to buy your sound.

Herc's black, Promethean appropriation of the two-
turntable technology of disco and his conversion of disco-
tech into a newly constructed blackurban form turned
the tables on analysts and market surveyors alike. For
competing disco DJs merely *blended* one disc into a suc-
cessor in order to keep the energized robots of a commercial style (not unlike Lambada) in perpetual motion on
the dance floor. *To disco* became a verb, but one without
verve to blackurban youth. What Herc, Flash, and their
cohort did was to actualize the immanent possibilities of
discotechnology. They turned two turntables into a
sound system through the technical addition of a beat
box, heavy amplification, headphones, and very, very
fast hands.

Why listen—the early hip hop DJs asked—to an entire commercial disc if the disc contained only twenty

(or two) seconds of worthwhile sound? Why not *work* that sound by having two copies of the same disc on separate turntables, moving the sound on the two tables in DJ-orchestrated patterns, creating thereby a worthwhile sound? The result was an indefinitely extendable, varied, reflexively signifying hip-hop sonics—indeed, a deft sounding of postmodernism.

The techniques of rap were not simply ones of selective extension and modification. They also included massive archiving. Black sound (African drums, bebop melodies, James Brown shouts, jazz improvs, Ellington riffs, blues innuendos, doo-wop croons, reggae words, calypso rhythms) were gathered into a reservoir of threads that DJs wove into intriguing tapestries of anxiety and influence. The word that comes to mind is *hybrid.*

Discotechnology was hybridized through the human hand and ear—the DJ turned wildman at the turntable. The conversion produced a rap DJ who became a postmodern ritual priest of sound rather than a passive spectator in an isolated DJ booth making robots turn. A reverse cyborgism was clearly at work in the rap conversion. The high technology of advanced sound production was reclaimed by and for human ears and the human body's innovative abilities. A hybrid sound then erupted in seemingly dead urban acoustical spaces. (By *postmodern* I intend the nonauthoritative collaging or archiving of sound and styles that bespeaks a deconstructive hybridity. Linearity and progress yield to a dizzying synchronicity.)

The Bronx, Brooklyn, Queens—called by the Reagan/Bush era black "holes" of urban blight—became concentrated masses of a new style, a hybrid sonics hip-hoppingly full of that piss, sass, and technological vinegar that tropes Langston Hughes, saying: *"I'm still here!"* This is a *blackhole* shooting hip, hop quasars and bum-rushing sucker, political DJs.

What time was it? Time to get busy from the midseventies into the wildstyle popularizations of the eighties. From Parks to Priority Records, from random sampling to Run DMC. Fiercely competitive and hugely braggadocious in their energies, the quest of the emergent rap technologists was for the baddest toasts, boasts, and signifying possible. The form was male-dominant—though KRS-One and the earliest male posses will tell you the "ladies" were *always* there. Answering back, dissing the ways of menfolk and kinfolk alike who tried to ease them into the postmodern dozens. Hey, Millie Jackson had done the voiceover with musical backdrop—had talked to wrongdoing menfolk (at length) before Run or Daryl had ever even figured out that some day they might segue into each other's voices talking 'bout some "dumb girl." Indeed!

↝   Rap technology includes *scratching:* rapidly moving the "wheels of steel" (i.e., turntables) back and forth with the disc cued, creating a deconstructed sound. There is *sampling:* taking a portion (phrase, riff, percussive vamp, etc.) of a known or unknown record (or a video game squawk, a touch-tone telephone medley, verbal tag from Malcolm X or Martin Luther King) and combining it in the overall mix. (The sample was called a *cut* in the earliest days.) *Punch phrasing:* to erupt into the sound of turntable #1 with a percussive sample from turntable #2 by def cuing.

But the most acrobatic of the technics is the verb and reverb of the human voice pushed straight out, or emulated by synthesizers, or emulating drums and falsettos, rhyming, chiming sound that is a mnemonic for black-urbanity.

The voice is individual talent holding the mike for as long as it can invoke and evoke a black tradition that is both prefabricated and in formation. "Yo, man, I hear Ellington, but you done put a new (W)rap on it!" For the rap to be defly *yours* and properly original, it has got to be *ours*—to sound like *us*.

The voice, some commentators have suggested, echoes African griots, black preachers, Apollo DJs, Birdland MCs, Muhammed Ali, black streetcorner males' signifying, oratory of the Nation of Islam, and get-down ghetto vernacular. The voice becomes the thing in which, finally, raptechnology catches the consciousness of the young.

What time is it? The beginning of the decade to end a century. It is postindustrial, drum machine, synthesizer, sampling, remix, multitrack studio time. But it is also a time in which *the voice*, and *the bodies* of rap and dance beat the rap of technologically induced (reproduced) indolence, impotence, or (in)difference.

Why?

Because sales figures are a mighty index. But also— the motion of the ocean of dancers who fill vast, olympian spaces of auditoriums and stadiums transnationally when you are (*à la* Roxanne) "live on stage" is still a principal measure of rap-success. Technology can create a rap disc, but only the voice dancing to wheels of steel and producing a hip-hopping, responsive audience gives testimony to a full-filled *break*. You ain't busted a move, in other words, until the audience lets you know you're in the groove.

What time is it? It's "hardcore" and "message" and "stop the violence" and "ladies first," 1990's time. Microcomputers, drum machines, electric keyboards, synthesizers are all involved in the audio. And MTV and the grammarians of the proper Grammy Awards have had their hands forced.

Rap is a too-energetic category for the Grammies to ignore, and Fab Five Freddy and "Yo! MTV Raps" have multiple billing these days. Jesse Jackson and Quincy Jones proclaim that "Rap is here to stay." Quincy has even composed and orchestrated a cross-generational album (*Back on the Block*) on which he announces his postmodernity in the sonics of rap. Ice-T and Big Daddy Kane prop him up "on every leaning side."

But it is also time to "fight the power" as Public Enemy knows—the power of media control. In their classic rap "Don't Believe the Hype," PE indicates that prime-time media is afraid of rap's message, considering it both offensive and dangerous. In Philadelphia, one of the principal popular music stations confirms PE's assessment. For WUSL ("Power 99") proudly advertises its "no-rap workday." Secretaries fill a sixty-second ad spot with kudos for the station's erasure of rap. Hence, FCC

"public" space is contoured in Philly in ways that erase
the energy of rap's soundings. *Work* (defined as tedious
office labor) is thus publicly constructed as incompatible
with *rap*. Ethics and outputs of wage-labor are held to
be incommensurate with postmodern black expressive
culture. Implicit in a *no-rap workday,* of course, is an
agon between industrial ("Taylorite") strategies of typing-
pool (Word Processing Pool?) efficiency and a radical
hybridity of sound and morals. For rap's sonics are disruptive in themselves. They become even more cacopho-
nous when they are augmented by the black voice's
anti-establishment injunctions, libido urgings, and
condemnations of coercive standardization. To "get the
job done" or "paid in full" in the economies of rap is
scarcely to sit for eight hours cultivating carpal tunnel
syndrome. Nope. To get the job done with rap style is
to "get busy," innovative, and outrageous with *fresh*
sounds and defiy nonstandard moves. One must be un-
disciplined, that is to say, to be "in effect."

Eric B. and Rakim, Redman, Twin Hype, BDP, Dig-
ital Underground, EPMD, De La Soul, Q-Tip, The
DOC—the names in themselves read like a Toni Mor-
rison catalogue of nonstandard cultural denomination.
And such named rap ensembles and the forms they produce are scarcely local or parochial. For rap has become
an international, metropolitan hybrid. From New Delhi
to Ibadan, it is busy interrupting the average workday.

Microcomputation, multitrack recording, video imaging, and the highly innovative vocalizations and chore-
ography of black urban youth have produced a form that

is fiercely intertextual, open-ended, hybrid. It has not only rendered melody virtually anomalous for any theory of "New Music," but also revised a current generation's expectations where "poetry" is concerned.

Technology's effect on student expectations and pedagogical requirements in, say, English literature classrooms is tellingly captured by recent experiences that I have had and would like to share. To prepare myself for a talk I was to give at New York's Poetry Project symposium entitled "Poetry for the Next Society" (1989) I decided to query students enrolled in a course devoted to Afro-American women writers. "What," I asked, "will be the poetry for the next society?" To a man or woman, my students responded "rap" and "MTV."

We didn't stop to dissect their claims, nor did we attempt a poetics of the popular. Instead, we tried to extrapolate from what seemed two significant forms of the present era a description of their being-in-the-world. Terms that emerged included: *public, performative, audible, theatrical, communal, intrasensory, postmodern, oral, memorable,* and *intertextual.* What this list suggests is that my students (yes, they were graduate students) believe the function of poetry belongs in our era to a telecommunal, popular space in which a global audience interacts with performative artists. A link between music and performance—specifically popular music and performance—seems determinative in their definition of the current and future function of poetry.

They are heirs to a history in which art, audience, entertainment, and instruction have assumed profoundly new meanings. The embodied catharsis of Dick Clark's

bandstand or Don Cornelius's soultrain would be virtually unrecognizable—or so one thinks—to Aristotle.
Thus, Elvis, Chuck Berry, and the Shirelles foreshadow
and historically overdetermine The Boss, Bobby Brown,
and Kool Moe Dee as, let us say, *People's Poets.*

My students' responses, however, are not nearly as
natural or original as they may seem on first view. In
fact, they have a familiar cast within a history of contestation and contradistinction governing the relationship
between poetry and the state.

The exclusion of poets from the republic by Plato is
the primary Western site of this contest. (One envisions
a no-poetry workday, as it were.) In Egypt it is Thoth
and the King; in Afro-America it is the Preacher and
the Bluesman. It would be overly sacramental to speak
of this contest as one between the letter and the spirit,
and it would be too Freudian by half to speak of it as a
struggle between the law and taboo. The simplest way
to describe it is in terms of a tensional resonance between homogeneity and heterogeneity.

Plato argues the necessity of a homogeneous state designed to withstand the bluesiness of poets who are always intent on worrying such a line by signifying and
troping irreverently on it and continually setting up con-
ditionals. "What if this?" and "What if that?" To have
a homogeneous line, Plato advocates that philosophers ef-
fectively eliminate poets. (Which is rather a forecast, I
think, of the Alan Bloom cry of the heart in our own
day.)

If the state is the site of what linguists call the *consta-
tive,* then poetry is an alternative space of the *conditional.*

If the state keeps itself in line, as Benedict Anderson suggests (and, yes, I did eventually get to read his book) through the linear, empty space of homogeneity, then poetry worries this space or line with heterogeneous performance. If the state is a place of reading the lines correctly, then poetry is the site of audition, of embodied sounding on state wrongs such as N.W.A's ". . . Tha Police," or PE's "Black Steel in the Hour of Chaos."

What, for example, happens to the state line about the death of the black family and the voiceless derogation of black youth when Run DMC explodes the state line with the rap: "Kings from Queens/ From Queens Come Kings/ We're Raising Hell Like a Class When the Lunch Bell Rings!/ Kings will be Praised/ And Hell Will Be Raised/ Suckers try to phase us/ But We Won't be phased!"

In considering the contest between homogeneity and heterogeneity, I am drawing on the work of the scholars Homi Bhabha and Peter Stallybrass, who suggest that nationalist or postrevolutionary discourse is always a discourse of the split subject. In order to construct the nation it is necessary to preserve a homogeneity of remembrance (such as anthems, waving flags, and unifying slogans) in conjunction with an amnesia of heterogeneity. If poetry, like rap, is disruptive performance or, in Homi Bhabha's formulation, an articulation of the melancholia of the people's wounding by and before the emergence of the state line, then poetry can be defined, again like rap, as an audible or sounding space of opposition. Rap is the form of audition in our present era that

utterly refuses to sing anthems of, say, STATE homogeneity.

A final autobiographical instance of rap-shifted student
expectations on the pedagogical front will conclude my
sounding of postmodernism. I recently (February 1990)
had the experience of crossing the Atlantic by night, followed by a metropolitan ride from Heathrow Airport
to North Westminster Community School in order to
teach Shakespeare's *Henry V* to a class of GCSE (General
Certificate of Secondary Education) students. Never
mind the circumstances occasioning the trip—no, on
second thought, the circumstances are popularly important.

A reporter for London's *The Mail on Sunday* had gotten onto the fact that I advocated rap as an absolute pre-
requisite for any teacher attempting to communicate
with students between the ages of twelve and twenty-
five. So there I was in London, in a school with students
representing sixty-seven nationalities and speaking twenty-two languages, in the Paddington/Marylebone area.
"Once more unto the breach, dear friends, once more;/
Or close the wall up with our English dead" was the passage the students were supposed to have concentrated
on, paying special attention to notions of "patriotism."

Introduced by the head of the English department to
a class doing everything but the postmodern boogie on
desktops, I pulled up a chair, sat down, and calmly
said: "I've come from the United States. I've been awake
for thirty-six hours, and I have to listen to you so that I
can answer questions from my teenage son about what

you are listening to, what you are *into*. So, please, start by telling me your names." Even as they began to give me their names (with varying degrees of cooperative audibility), a black British young woman was lining up twelve rap cassette boxes on her desk immediately in front of me. (Hey, she knew I had *nothing* to teach her!)

To make an exciting pedagogical story brief, we took off—as a group. I showed them how Henry V was a rapper—a cold dissing, def con man, tougher-than-leather and smoother-than-ice, an artisan of words. His response to the French Dauphin's gift of tennis balls was my first presentational text. And then—"the breach." We did that in terms of a fence in the yard of a house that you have just purchased. A neighbor breaches it— "How, George? How could your neighbor breach it?" George jerked up from that final nod that would have put him totally asleep and said, "What?" "Could your neighbor do anything to breach your fence, George?" "No, Sir, I don't think so." "Come on, George!" "Sir . . . Oh, yeah, he could break it."

And then the anterior question about "breaches" and "fences" was arrived at by another student, and I leaped out of my chair in congratulation. "Sir, the first question is 'Why was the fence there in the first place?'" Right! What time was it?

It was time for Public Enemy's "Don't Believe the Hype." Because all of that Agincourt admonition and "breach" rhetoric (the whole hybrid, international class of London GCSE students knew) was a function of the English Church being required to pay the king "in

full," and the state treasury could only get the duckets
if ancient (and spurious) boundary claims are made to
send Henry V and the boys into somebody else's yard.
Patriotism, a show of hands by the class revealed, is a
"hype" if it means dying for England. Bless his soul,
though, there was one stout lad who held up his hand
and said he would be ready to die for England. My
black British young lady, who had put her tapes away,
shouted across the room, "That's because you're English!"

Hybridity: a variety of sounds coming together to
arouse interest in a classic work of Shakespearean creation.

The *Mail on Sunday* reporter told me as we left North
Westminster that the English department head had
asked her to apologize to me in advance for the GCSE
group because they would never listen to what I had to
say and would split the room *as soon as the bell rang.* (Actually, eight or nine of the students surrounded me after
class seeking, as they put it, "scholarships" to go back
with me to America—"now, Sir!")

What the head had not factored into her apologetics
was the technology I came bearing. I carried along my
very own Panasonic cassette blaster as the postmodern
analogue of both "the message" and the "rapper's delight" that Shakespeare himself would include in his
plays were he writing today. At a site of postmodern,
immigrant, sonic (twenty-two languages) hybridity produced by an internationally accessible technology, I
gained pedagogical entree by playing in the new and
very, very sound game of rap.

Like Jesse, I believe rap is here to stay. Other forms such as "house" and "hip-house" and "rap reggae" may spin off, but rap is now classical black sound. It is the "in effect" archive where postmodernism has been dopely sampled for the international nineties. It is the job of Black Studies to provide an adequate hearing.

AFTERWORD

The maze of temporal and scholarly difficulties that confronted me during the summer of 1991 has not, unfortunately, become simpler during the past year. Not only is there more to be accounted for in the black popular sphere, but also an abundance of bad news from the inner-city home front. If rap geographies have become younger with the appearance of such performers as ABC and TLS and more womanistly militant with Sister Souljah, then inner-city economies have become ever more perilous. The extraordinary acquittal of four Los Angeles policemen who were videotaped in that act of mercilessly beating the black Rodney G. King produced fires of rage in South Central Los Angeles and across the United States in April of 1992. Violence, looting, and arson broke out in Seattle, Las Vegas, Atlanta, and San Francisco. More than fifty deaths and innumerable assaults and injuries occurred in Los Angeles alone. The mean, white gloating, faintly amused faces of the attorneys for the acquitted white policemen and the spotted, angular, thin-haired visage of the former Los Angeles chief of police, Daryl Gates, are frightening reminders of bitter times past.

It is difficult to understand how any black person of the least privilege can fail to be appalled by the unfolding of the Rodney King tragedy. And how can anyone who is academically well placed doubt that only Black Studies in its myriad American imbrications, comprehensiveness of analysis, and rigorous historical grounding can begin to construct an adequate framework for today's complex black American situation?

The beating of Rodney King—an American citizen already grounded and struggling to keep an arm or a leg in motion in order to remain conscious enough to try to avoid the next baton blow—is the image of the late-twentieth-century. Rich, cynical white citizens and their henchmen are everywhere pounding the hell out of "the rest of us" average Americans. "They get the justice in the end," one might say, "and they come by tens!"

Most of the population of the United States is financially hard-pressed, crippled by the absence of justice in everyday life, and distressingly aware that an unseemly white-male profittaking during the 1980s has brought the United States to the precipice of human disaster. If there is a general, public, oppositional response to such obscenity, then surely one of its most energetic sites is the black inner city. The inner city provides today not only oppositional masses, but also the style, tone, themes, and lyrics for at least one international sounding of American reality that has rocked the world: rap.

If it is rap and its creators, distributors, and individual geniuses who have continued the voluble beat of the inner-city blues from the 1960s, then surely there are ample scholarly reasons for us to look to the form's sonics for ethical reinforcement. Black Studies engages rap at the site of the academy in order to begin a cultural studies project that may, if we are extraordinarily lucky and courageous, get us on our feet again, out of the immediate reach of swinging batons we did not simply *think* we saw, but actually *did* see with the clarity of a national disaster.

A new story of Black Studies is part of the mandatory academic work of rewriting, reversing, or forestalling— at least for the foreseeable future—what Blanchot calls the "catastrophe." It seems high time, then, for those of us who are inside to get seriously busy about the business of Black Studies for the nineties—to bust a move and rigorously bring the scholarly noise for a new generation.

INDEX

Index

Index

TLS, 101
Tone-Lōc, 48, 49, 51, 53, 55*il*
Toop, David, 80, 86
Too Short, 57
Twin Hype, 93
2 Live Crew, 51, 52, 53, 56, 57, 58, 64, 67, 69, 71–75

Unity Day, 3–5, 4*il,* 29–32
University. *See also* Academy: and black liberation, 9, 10; changing admissions standards, 14; democratizing of, 8; exclusivity of, 8; police presence at, 21; private, 7; radicalizing of, 9–15; as site of resistance, 8; state, 7; symbolic militancy, 15; territorial conflict in, 15–16; and Western knowledge indoctrination, 7, 8, 15, 28

Vaux, Calvert, 40
Victimization: in Central Park Jogger case, 51; young, black, male, 34

Violence, 101; eradication of, 74; male, 72; and patriarchy, 67; against women, 50–52, 73–74

Walker, Alice, 2
West, Cornel, 27, 69
Wilding, 46, 47, 48, 50, 51, 58
"Wild Thing," 49, 52
Will, George, 51–53
Witnessing, expert, 61–84; instant, 79–82; to popular cultural forms, 68–69; self-aggrandizement in, 81–83
Women's Liberation, 16, 71
Women's Studies, 16, 17
Wright, Richard, 56

X-ing, 35, 36

Yale University, 22
"Yo! MTV Raps" (television), 3, 92
Young MC, 49

Zanger, Mark, 65, 67–68, 79, 80

01952
605513